Am I Called To Be a
CHAPLAIN

CHAPLAIN PATTY

ISBN:

Book Writer Online
5 Oak, Creek Drive,
Buffalo Grove, IL 60089

www.bookwriteronline.com

DEDICATION & APPRECIATION

God inspired me to write this in hopes that others will understand the mission chaplains are called to. I could not have done it without Him. He led me, He trained me and gave me resources that I can now share with you because God has an assignment for you to reach people that might never hear about His goodness. I dedicate this book to my Lord and Savior, Jesus Christ.

I also want to say thank you to Dr. Barbara Odom. Not only is she my spiritual mother, but she also encouraged me to write this book and helped me in the writing of it.

CONTENTS

PREFACE

After selling my business, I moved from the business of Southern California to Mohave County in the beautiful deserts of Arizona. I thought I was moving there to retire but God had other plans. After my husband passed away God opened an opportunity for me to receive my license as an ordained minister/chaplain, and then He opened a door to chaplaincy. I stepped through that door not knowing what was to come, but I trusted the Lord.

I learned that chaplains have similarities with other ministers, but also many differences as well. I wanted to understand the differences of chaplaincy work and in understanding the varieties of chaplains then that would help me to grow into the kind of chaplain God called me to be.

Training was provided at my local church for Disaster Relief Chaplains, and I knew I needed that course. After that I took many more courses, some online and some in other cities, and each one helped me to build the knowledge I needed to serve as a Disaster Chaplain. Although saddened by the tragic events, it's also been very rewarding.

In addition to being sent out on disasters I've also spent time serving people in convalescent homes, visiting with people one on one, praying for them, and teaching the word in a group setting. That too has been very rewarding.

I believe this book will help you to also understand the varieties of chaplaincy and perhaps you'll find where you fit and where God can best use the gifts, He created you with. My hopes are that you'll make yourself available to the need.

CHAPTER 1
WHAT IS A CHAPLAIN'S LIFE AND MINISTRY?

Chaplains and pastors share many tasks and abilities. Both have experienced a special call to ministry and service. Many chaplains are teachers, caregivers, witnesses of their faith, and advocates for people. Very similar to the calling of a local pastor. Both have the desire to equip people to grow in spiritual maturity. So, what's the difference? The most significant difference is the setting in which the ministry is provided.

Chaplains are clergy members from a myriad of various religious faiths who have chosen to minister to people outside the walls of a church or other house of worship. They can be volunteers or employed by an institution or agency and serve the institution's clients, employees, and families. From a Christian perspective, their role is pastoral, prophetic, and priestly, even while simply talking to those who profess no religion, and sometimes no God. They enter the ministry opportunity with no personal agenda and the attitude of a servant.

Here are a few verses that will help you to understand why we are chaplains because there's so much more to being a chaplain than having a card in your wallet.

Reading out of the NLT Bible Jesus told us in Luke 10:27 "You must love the Lord your God with all your heart, all your soul, all your strength, and all your mind.' And, 'Love your neighbor as yourself.'"

A chaplain is representing Jesus as His ambassador, and love is the culture. Therefore, you want to be the best you, by God's grace. Once you were born again, you changed citizenships. Consequently, you are not of this world, and you don't live like the world, or act like the world. You're of a different Kingdom.

Jesus continues the conversation and gives us a mandate through this parable found in Luke 10:29-37 NLT:

The man wanted to justify his actions, so he asked Jesus, "And who is my neighbor?" Jesus replied with a story: "A Jewish man was traveling from Jerusalem down to Jericho, and he was attacked by bandits. They stripped him of his clothes, beat him up, and left him half dead beside the road.

"By chance a priest came along. But when he saw the man lying there, he crossed to the other side of the road and passed him by. A Temple assistant walked over and looked at him lying there, but he also passed by on the other side. "Then a despised Samaritan came along, and when he saw the man, he felt compassion for him.

Going over to him, the Samaritan soothed his wounds with olive oil and wine and bandaged them. Then he put the man on his own donkey and took him to an inn, where he took care of him. The next day he handed the innkeeper two silver coins, telling him, 'Take care of this man. If his bill runs higher than this, I'll pay you the next time I'm here.'

"Now which of these three would you say was a neighbor to the man who was attacked by bandits?", Jesus asked. The man replied, "The one who showed him mercy." Then Jesus said, "Yes, now go and do the same."

We take the time to love people right where they are and we do so not expect anything in return. That was the heart of the good Samaritan and that should be the heart of every chaplain.

As Christian chaplains, we love peace, and model it. We do our best to not get angry and we never promote or escalate conflict during a crisis. It is not about you and your political opinions; it's all about Jesus and the person, or people you're serving at the moment. Again, you represent Jesus when you stand in the office as a chaplain. *"A church leader (or chaplain) is a manager of God's household (or people), so he must live a blameless life. He must not be arrogant or quick-tempered; he must not be a heavy drinker, violent, or dishonest with money."* Titus 1:7

Chaplains do not take their assignment lightly. We must be honorable to the Lord when we accept this calling. If you're married, please be faithful to your spouse. If you're single, remain faithful to the Lord avoiding sexual promiscuity. When you step into the ministry of chaplaincy you must remember you are a servant of the Lord and you're His ambassador, representing Him, the Body of Christ (aka: the Church) and the Kingdom of God.

When it comes to drinking alcohol, it might be a controversial subject but what I need to address is the problem of drinking heavily. I recommend that you don't drink at all because it will affect your ability to answer emergency calls if your blood alcohol level is too high. However, if you do drink alcohol please do so in moderation.

While we're talking about substances it's vital that you do not use illegal or addictive drugs. It would be disconcerting to you, and to the ministry you represent, if you arrived on the scene of a tragedy and were arrested because you were intoxicated. It would be detrimental if you were en route to a crisis and were in a car accident where someone might be killed or badly hurt because you were under the influence. That unfortunate scenario would bring a reproach on the ministry and the body of Christ.

A Chaplain's Life of Helping Others

As our love grows for the Lord Jesus Christ, so does our passion for helping others. We understand it's not about works, it's about the love God has shown us, and now He's asking us to show others that same love through good works. He'll develop compassion in us and give us the ability to serve others in their time of need. I like the way Lauren Cunningham, (the founder of Youth with a Mission) said it, "We want to know God and make Him known".

Even though there is no official word for "chaplain" in the Bible, the parable of the Good Samaritan, that we already referred to, gives us the base on which we stand.

The Samaritan had a servant's heart and that's the heart that God puts in a chaplain. This man was probably as busy as the others, but he stopped what he was doing to help another man in need. In doing so, you take up your cross and follow Jesus. *"And He said to them all 'if any man will come after Me, let him deny himself, take up his cross daily, and follow Me'." Luke 9:23*

A Chaplain's Life of Learning

"A wise man will hear and will increase learning; a man of understanding shall attain unto wise counsels." Proverbs 1:5

The more you follow this path to chaplaincy the more you'll find you need to learn. It's never as fast as you'd like it to be because transformation takes time. It will be imperative to get some training and understand your role as a chaplain and how to be sensitive to people's spiritual, emotional, and physical needs. Some areas of chaplaincy will be heart wrenching and then there will be other capacities in which you'll serve, that are relatively easy. But you'll always be affected by what you see and hear.

There are a variety of avenues for training. Your pastor might, or might not, be able to train you because they might not be proficient themselves in chaplaincy. Their expertise is shepherding sheep, discipling others, being at the pulpit teaching in ministry, studying and praying, and administrating the business of a church. Not everyone is gifted to be an *"Apostle, Prophet, Evangelist, Pastor or Teacher" Ephesians 4:11-13* and the giftings needed to be an effective chaplain will vary. The bottom line is Jesus has put each person in the body of Christ as He sees fit, and He will lead you to resources where you can be trained well for what He's asked you to do.

When you do find the training needed take it slow and understand what you're learning. There are so many areas that a chaplain can work in, and you need to understand where you belong, which could take a little time. If God has called you, He will equip you and help you find the people that will help you grow.

International Critical Incident Stress Foundation (ICISF) has excellent training. It is used by various

Religious Denominations, Police Departments, Paramedics, Fire Departments, City Councils, Counties, States, Federal Governments, and more. ICISF is across our nation for diverse trainings including special training for chaplains. Their contact information is:

International Critical Incident Stress Foundation, Inc
3290 Pine Orchard Lane, Suite 106
Ellicott City, MD 21042
www.icisf.org (410)750-9600 info@icisf.org

Mickey Stonier is an excellent teaching Chaplain for ICISF, and I have taken two of his courses. He's generally on the West Coast of the USA, but also teaches throughout the nation and has also taught ICISF courses in the beautiful land of Ireland. He is from the San Diego area of California and is the head chaplain in the denomination he belongs to, teaching other chaplains. I highly recommend any class he teaches however you'll find all the courses are excellent.

In chaplaincy you'll crawl before you walk, and you'll walk before you run. There's a reason for "baby steps". Just one step at a time and *"God will complete the good work He began in you" Philippians 1:6.*

The reason it takes time to develop as a chaplain is because you must learn to understand the nature of human beings and how to help in a crisis. Some areas you will serve in could make you throw up your hands and say, "I can't do this". The tragedies that take place in humanity will affect you psychologically and you must be prepared to handle the emotional roller coaster you might find yourself on. Some chaplains can help a person at the end of their life on a daily or weekly basis, and they're good at it. The chaplain is able to work through the pain in their own heart as that person passes away. However, there are other chaplains that would not be able to handle that kind of ministry but would be very effective in another type of service helping people.

Earning a degree is not as important as the anointing you have to do what God's called you to do. But you can have both if you so desire. As you renew your mind to the Word of God you will be equipped for every good work. Don't neglect your times of devotion with the Lord. Take your Bible, read it, journal what God is saying to you through His Word and talk to Him. He has the answers you're looking for.

When I earned a private pilot's license, it was a license to learn. It is the same as a chaplain/minister getting their license before they are ordained; although you've already gone through the process of ministerial preparation your first license is a step to learn more. You never stop learning as a pilot and you always continue learning as a chaplain or a minister. Stay humble. As a pilot, you can't get too cocky, or you'll get into trouble and probably crash. The same is true in ministry.

Some start ministry for the Lord early in their life, and the rest of us start a little late in life. But God knew exactly where we would be at this time. Therefore, take your time, but keep moving forward. We are all different because we all reach different people. Not one person or one personality can reach every person in the world. Even in Jesus' hometown, people didn't always listen to Him or even believe that He was, and is, the Son of God.

"And they were offended by him. But Jesus said unto them, 'A prophet is not without honor, save in his own country and house.' And He did not many mighty works there because of their unbelief." Matthew 13:57-58.

Remember, as the chaplain, you are the minister on the scene. Therefore, you need to have knowledge. *Proverbs 17:27 says "A man of understanding is of an excellent spirit"* and *Proverbs 4:7 says "with all thy getting, get understanding".* So where do we get understanding? We get it from trusting in God's Word. *Proverbs 3:5 tells us "Trust in the Lord with all your heart and lean not to your own understanding".*

You'll need this understanding to be a better listener and a better encouragement to people. Even if you officiate weddings, and funerals, or a service in a convalescent home.

7

Sometimes you'll minister one-on-one and other times in small groups, or even large groups. But you'll always need wisdom and understanding in every situation. *"For the Lord giveth wisdom: out of his mouth cometh knowledge and understanding."* Proverbs 2:6

Education in this field will help you to understand the way in which we should approach the hurting during a disaster. It revolves around the understanding of how people can react to different situations and how we can reach out more effectively with compassion.

A Chaplains Life of Receiving Wisdom

At the beginning of your ministry as a chaplain you will be assigned to various areas of ministry. Learn to use wisdom in that area. Then you'll repeat that process as you move to different areas of ministry until you find yourself in the chaplaincy God has gifted you for. *"Wisdom is the principal thing; therefore, get wisdom: and with all thy getting get understanding." Proverbs 4:7*

I'm aware that not every person reading this book is of the Pentecostal persuasion but if you do pray in the Spirit then make sure you pray in the Spirit and also in your understanding before you minister to someone. If you don't pray in tongues, then please pray in your native language. Perhaps on the way to the crisis is your best time of prayer. You'll receive wisdom from the Lord for each individual you minister to.

When you speak to a person you'll speak with understanding. Don't use words that the average person might not understand. Speak in terms that a 10-year-old could understand. Remember, others are listening too, such as family members, and they need to comprehend what you're saying as well.

As a chaplain, you will be speaking to people from all denominations, or movements. Whatever faith you are as a chaplain, don't use this as an opportunity to drive your denomination's theology. I enjoy ministering to people when we share the same beliefs, but it doesn't always work out that way. You're there to give them comfort and love to each person, like Jesus would.

A Chaplain's Life of Prayer

"And He spoke a parable unto them to this end, that man ought always to pray, and not to faint." Luke 18:1

It's imperative that you pray about everything, because there will be opportunities to "faint" when serving people in this line of ministry.

As a minister, serving people you'll find you're in a spiritual battle. Prayer and meditating on the Word are a few of your spiritual weapons. *"Submit to God, resist the devil and he will flee from you" (James 4:7)*. This verse gives you something to do in spiritual battle. And if you do these two things you will overcome. Prayer does make a difference.

There is an enemy, the devil. *"He came not but for to steal, kill and destroy" (John 10:10)*, so he will try to stop you because he wants to destroy you and others. The Bible tells us to *"Be sober, be vigilant; because your adversary, the devil, as a roaring lion, walketh about, seeking whom he may devour:" 1 Peter 5:8*.

"You are more than a conqueror" Romans 8:37 and have the victory over the enemy. But you come to know that through prayer, Bible study and meditating on the Word of God. Trusting in what He says to you. The word of God is our Sword, our offense and our defense. *"Put on the whole armor of God so you can stand against all evil." Ephesians 6:11*

The devil will try to use our past sins to bring shame. He's known as the accuser of the brethren. He will try to use bad habits and bitterness that we once held in our hearts by lying to our minds. We must remember that God no longer sees our past sins when confess Jesus as our Lord. He washed them with the blood of His Son and removed them far from us. The blood of Jesus is greater than any sin we've ever committed. Past, present, or future.

This is why Paul warned every believer to take every thought captive to the obedience of Christ. *"Casting down imaginations, and every high thing that exalteth itself against the knowledge of God, and bringing into captivity every thought to the obedience of Christ." 2 Corinthians 10:5*

Your faith will grow strong as you spend time in prayer and the Word and it will be important to you when you're agreeing in prayer with someone that is walking through a crisis. *"But let him ask in faith, nothing wavering. For he that wavereth is like a wave of the sea driven with the wind and tossed." (James 1:6)*

Faith and belief come from the Greek word "pistis," which means to trust. So, we need to trust Him. We can't change anything or anyone, but God can through His Son, Jesus Christ. *"Therefore, I say unto you, what things soever ye desire when ye pray, believe that ye receive them, and ye shall have them." (Mark 11:24)*

Don't pray last, pray first. You can communicate with your Lord and Savior regularly, so stay prayed up. Once you've prayed you can be confident that God will answer.

"And this is the confidence that we have in Him that, if we ask anything according to His will, He hears us. And if we know that He hears us, whatever we ask, we know that we have the petitions we have asked of Him." 1 John 5:14-15

You can receive revelation of what Holy Spirit wants to do in every situation. What's important is that you pray and you listen to what Holy Spirit is saying. Be sincere, not praying vain repetitious prayers full of fluff and no faith.

"But when ye pray, use not vain repetitions, as the heathen do, for they think that they shall be heard for their much speaking. Be not ye, therefore, like unto them: for your Father knoweth what things ye need of before ye ask Him." Matthew 6:7-8

In one of the courses I took with chaplains from all denominations we were to simulate a police officer that had to shoot somebody in the line of duty. It affects officers even when it's a necessary shooting of a human being. We were asked to pretend that we were the chaplain, talking to the police officer, to help him process emotionally what happened.

The person I was working with immediately asked me why I was not talking instantly. I said I was waiting for the Holy Spirit to lead me. And her words were, "you don't have time for that, you need to start speaking right now". But my belief is that right now, I better take time to listen to the Holy Spirit. I don't want to say the wrong words at a time like this and just be talking. Sometimes our presence will be enough. A good rule of thumb is "no comments are better than wrong comments". The Bible says:

"When we tell you these things, we do not use words that come from human wisdom. Instead, we speak words given to us by the Spirit, using the Spirit's words to explain spiritual truths." 1 Corinthians 2:13 NLT

"But the Comforter, which is the Holy Ghost, whom the Father will send in my name, shall teach you all things, and bring all things to your remembrance, whatsoever I have said unto you." John 14:26

A Chaplain's Life of Compassion

Compassion and respect will help give you a good understanding of those you serve, patience to wait for an invitation, and an ability to have a humble spirit. Even though the chaplain is a representative for God, the chaplain is not, and never will be God. As such, the chaplain cannot decide for anyone how to think, believe, or act. Even Jesus did not force others to follow him. The chaplain must demonstrate compassion for all persons by first sharing love in action. Talk to people, listen to them, and pray for them. Then you can share the truth of the Word when invited to.

The Biblical basis for Christians to pursue chaplaincy answers the basic question of why chaplain ministry is implemented. From the mandates *"to go"* and *"to serve the least of these,"* chaplains understand that they minister to all people, regardless of age, gender, ethnicity, or faith tradition. Chaplains understand that the ministry of "showing up" is sometimes the ministry most needed. From the directive to feed, clothe, shelter, visiting the prisoner to visiting those that are sick, chaplains understand that practical acts of service are vital to demonstrating faith in God. And from the examples of Jesus, Paul, Tabitha, Martha and more, chaplains recognize the importance of respecting differences in culture and faiths, always providing opportunities for people to hopefully choose Jesus.

The first element of a practical, compassionate person is just being present. Sometimes in traumatic situations, chaplains can be intimidated by the magnitude of the crisis and they're not certain how to respond to a person in need. Even though some chaplains might need more professional training they also might be the ones that give the most compassionate care. Being present with someone in a crisis is often 90% of what is needed. Your response can make things better or worse, and there are moments when it is best to remain silent rather than fill in time with empty words.

Being present is a privilege, not a right. And in working with survivors, one must remember that the physical presence of a chaplain is not helpful if it is not wanted. The chaplain must understand that they have no right to enter the world of another's pain without invitation.

Sometimes, survivors may strike out with intense emotions at those trying to help. Chaplains who recognize anger as a secondary emotion and look at the hurt, fear and frustration underlining the more visible expression of those feelings will be more likely to respond with love and compassion. The effective chaplain will be slow to speak and acutely aware of the power of a calm, non-anxious person, expecting to come alongside and be a welcomed help of kindness.

It is essential to note that sometimes even seasoned chaplains feel a profound sense of inadequacy and failure because we're not able to help every person in need. However, a peaceful, comforting presence for someone is irreplaceable when there are no words. Although it can be a struggle for some to learn to be comfortable in silence.

Affective emotional and spiritual care must also be

practical and will often be most accepted and helpful when assisting a survivor with the tasks of everyday life. Meeting practical needs is an important part of ministry.

Chaplains are defined as being continually influenced by relationships. Almost all of what you do flows from who you are and in order to help a person facing a disaster we must connect emotionally and spiritually. Relationships are the essence of existence, and the core of our humanity is that we develop relationships with others.

A Chaplain's Life with Family

Don't be offended if close family and friends don't respect you as a chaplain. They often remember who you were "before Christ" and wonder how you could possibly help them, or even others. Remember it's not what you did in your past that qualifies you but what you do in your present and in your future. In time your family and friends will see that Jesus has changed you from the inside out; thank God we're not the people we used to be, *"old things have passed away"*.

A Chaplain's Life of Cultural Change

The chaplain's traditional role is comparable to the position of the clergy in most religious communities. The English word 'pastor' means shepherd, one who cares for a flock. Thus, the chaplain's pastoral role may incorporate many spiritual-care ministries to manage and nurture people and their situations. These spiritual-care ministries could include the classic and contemporary approaches; scriptural instruction, interpretation, prayer, meditation, spiritual direction, presence, listening, and reflection.

As a chaplain, you will be ministering to people from all denominations. Be ethical when if you're in a group, giving a sermon. I am Pentecostal, and I love the Pentecostal ways. However, if I'm with a group of those that don't believe the way I do, then I'll never be talking about praying in tongues. There are many scriptural passages that we do agree on across denominational lines, so share something from one of those passages, as the Lord leads of course. Every service in the community is non-denominational and the Word can reach every person of every faith by the power of His Spirit.

You'll also be serving people from all denominations when you're out in the field, and some won't even be saved. So, stay in the boundaries of the word of God. Don't change the Bible because it is THE truth and *"He is the same yesterday, today, and forever" Hebrews 13:8.* Stand on the word and be loving and kind as you present the uncompromised Word of God.

A Chaplain's Life of Changing Terms.

Because of spiritual care in our nation's ever-increasing religious diversity, the language of chaplaincy is changing. At one time, the preferred term was "pastoral care." Later "pastoral care" seemed too Christian and narrow in scope. The more acceptable term in the secular world is now "spiritual care," and chaplains now work in Spiritual Care Departments.

A Chaplain's Life of Religious Diversity.

Chaplains understand that they initiate ministry to all people, regardless of age, gender, ethnicity, or faith tradition. Chaplains recognize the importance of respecting differences in culture and religion, always allowing people to choose their paths, in hopes that they choose Jesus.

And if they don't choose Jesus, you are there for comfort. Be kind with your words. Don't be argumentative about their beliefs because God gives every person a free choice. If they see kindness from you, it could bring them to the Lord at a later time. Just plant the seed; someone else will water it, and someone else will harvest the soul.

A Chaplain's Life During Pandemics

As I'm writing this book I'm sitting in my home on Good Friday, April 10, 2020. A virus called "Covid 19" is sweeping through many nations. It has brought some people together, and others have been made to feel forgotten and still other families have been torn apart. Yet the chaplains work has been halted. There are no visitors or ministers to those in convalescent homes or hospitals. Chaplains are told to not tend to those found in crisis or disaster to protect their own health as well as the health of others. The world is "locked-down".

Some do not have a faith in God that they can draw on while in physical pain. Hospitals are locked down except for emergency care. So many are in pain and cannot get the help they need. Many of us chaplains are staying in contact with people, either by phone or face calls with computers or phones. Because of the technological changes our world has gone through in the last decade we have access to people if we'll simply use it. In doing so we can pray for people and continue to take them to the Lord in prayer, once the conversation has ended.

A pandemic also brings a lot of governmental issues and praying for our leaders in government is more important now than it's ever been. During the terrorist act of 9/11, so many people started praying for our country, but many did not continue. We're in a war in our nation between Godly values and the spirit of the anti-Christ. Chaplains and Christians alike should be praying for our leaders. Pray in your understanding and if you pray in the Spirit, then do so. Allow Holy Spirit to pray the perfect will of God using you.

A Chaplain's Life of Preparation

Prepare yourself physically and mentally. Our bodies belong to the Lord, and His service, so we must care for them. It will take discipline to exercise and eat right. To keep our minds alert and be emotionally healthy. If you take care of yourself, you'll be able to care for others. Prepare to be on your feet 8-10 hours daily and always be ready physically for disaster at a moment's notice.

Prepare to dress appropriately when you're on the field

or serving people in need. As an example, disaster relief groups have a uniform t-shirt. It identifies you as someone that has been trained and confirmed as a chaplain. However, when you go into a convalescent home or the hospital, you don't have a uniform, so dress modestly. If you're a woman, avoid showing cleavage, avoid shorts or short skirts and avoid tight clothing. This will keep a person's focus on what you're saying, not what you're revealing about yourself.

Prepare a small stuffed animal or toy that you can give to a child to help calm them emotionally after a disaster or a crisis at hand. In fires, tornadoes, floods and hurricanes the children have lost everything. So, a stuffed animal might be a welcomed gesture of kindness and thoughtfulness.

Prepare a list of agency numbers, either in your smart phone or a card that you can refer to.

Prepare yourself for debriefing. You'll need another chaplain, pastor or counselor that you can share your feelings with regarding the crisis you just assisted in. It will help you to cope mentally. Sometimes you'll experience compassion fatigue where you are so exhausted emotionally and physically that it diminishes your ability to empathize or feel compassion towards another person. So, prepare yourself for what is to come.

Many people find the Serenity Prayer helpful, "God grant me the serenity to accept the things I cannot change, courage to change the things I can, and the wisdom to know the difference."

You'll also need to be prepared to periodically officiate a wedding, a funeral, or a service in a convalescent home. Have preferred wedding vows ready, a preferred funeral eulogy and a preferred messaged to teach if called upon.

"Moreover, because the preacher was wise, he still taught the people knowledge; yea, he gave good heed, and sought out, and set in order many proverbs." Ecclesiastes 12

CHAPTER 2
A CHAPLAIN AND DISCRETION

Proverbs 2:11 tells us, *"Discretion will guard you"*. According to the Online Dictionary discretion means: the quality of behaving or speaking in such a way as to avoid causing offense or revealing private information, and discretion is crucial for chaplains, and should be for all Christians.

Chaplains will be in many tough situations that will require us to think before we speak. I, for one, have not always used discretion in my speaking but I've repented for that and moved on. If everything depends on you then you'll find you won't always have the right answers. But you have a Helper, the Holy Spirit. If you'll listen to Him, He'll give you the right words to say at the right time and present it in the right way.

You'll be asked questions like, 'How could God have let this happen?', and the best thing that you can say is 'I don't know' because we really don't. As a chaplain serving disaster victims, you are there to comfort the victims and show Jesus' love.

One thing I often say to the victims who are Christians is; "you have such a wonderful Christian family, and your church is there with you during this time, let them help you". Because I believe that God will turn this around for their good. But the devastation is overwhelming at the time and it's hard to see past 'today'.

When you meet victims who are unbelievers, they often ask "If God is everything everybody says then He would not have let this happen". At this point, you're probably going to have to say the same thing "I don't know why this happened. But I do know God loves you and He cares about you". You're not pushing them away; you're just sharing the love of God. That's compassion.

In showing compassion avoid saying you know how they feel because the odds are you don't really know. I know a few chaplains who have lost everything in fire or floods, and they do understand. However, the person you're talking to thinks nobody understands what they're going through. Why? Because every person deals with a disaster differently.

In being led by Holy Spirit on the choice of your words does it matter if the person is a Christian or non-Christian? An atheist or an agnostic? A Jew, Muslim or Buddhist? Straight of LGBTQAI? Every person is going through devastation, and everyone is hurting. Sometimes you're standing in front of a person, not saying anything, but you're listening to Holy Spirit, who has made His home in you, and He gave you a word to give to somebody else in need. Be the vessel available to be used by the Lord.

CHAPTER 3
KNOW ABOUT PTSD

Post-Traumatic Stress Disorder can affect anyone, not just war veterans. Emergency Medical Technicians (EMTs) see disasters and death sometimes daily, and many experience PTSD because of their work. Even a smell or sound can set off PTSD. It can cause anxiety, major depression, substance abuse, and suicide in EMT's more than the general population, according to scientific studies in the US and England. The stressful situations EMT's experience can also increase the risk of physical health problems and complications. These first responders' function on a small amount of sleep during long shifts. However, the pressure of life and death hangs over every action that they experience—witnessing traumatic events regularly as lasting and re-occurring effects on the brain. More than ever, they need God to show them how to handle this mental conflict.

Many times, our police officers have a problem getting help because of the position of their role as a public authority. We need to pray for those in authority and be available as a chaplain to listen to our officers and give words of encouragement when invited to. Be a chaplain to them, someone who will listen and pray.

People from all walks of life can struggle with PTSD. Anyone that has experienced trauma or crisis can have fear attack them and they might struggle emotionally eating at a restaurant in peace, or struggle to enjoy going to the movie theatre with their family. Because of the recent pandemic some fear getting close enough to people to shake their hand or give a brother a hug. Chaplains are present to bring an ear to listen and a calm word from the Lord as we pray for others.

Many disaster scenes can cause PTSD. A car accident, when one barely escapes their house fire, an earthquake, hurricane, flood, or tornado. Every human being can be affected by this harassing mental and emotional disorder and must know how to navigate it.

I have a friend that shared her story of a slight case of PTSD. She had been through a disaster relief training herself and knew the symptoms of PTSD and so was aware when it happened.

She had been in a car accident with her grown daughter who was the mother of her four grandchildren. A tour bus had run them off the road when she tried to pass him, and her car spun in the desert sand. She knows it must have been guardian angels that protected them from flipping the car over and possibly killing or injuring them both.

After the accident she found she couldn't make simple decisions like what kind of shampoo to purchase, how much food to prepare, or whether to drive to church or not. She struggled passing any bus or truck wondering if she was making a life-altering decision for her, and her family that would be affected by the loss.

It took time but she submitted her symptoms to the Lord and He walked her through this healing of anxiety and she's completely free of PTSD today.

Just as she was delivered from PTSD as a chaplain, or even as a Christian, you can help people receive their healing from PTSD. You might have weaknesses yourself but even in your weakness Jesus is made strong. Help people understand that God is always on their side. Ask the Holy Spirit to lead you and you'll have wisdom in the words He gives you. Step lightly because sometimes it's hard for people to understand how God can help them and you might not understand what they're going through, but *the love of God has been poured in your heart by Holy Spirit. And love never fails.*

Don't be pushy or condescending, sometimes people have trust issues because of their experiences. When people are talking with you, keep it confidential, be discreet, never repeat what they say to anyone. Besides the legal matter of confidentiality, you're building trust.

CHAPTER 4
CHAPLAINS & SUICIDE PREVENTION

According to recent studies suicide rates increase by 62% in the first year after an earthquake, 31% in the first two years after a hurricane, and almost 14% four years after a flood. It can be devastating when a person has lost everything. So as a chaplain, we need to be on the lookout for suicidal statements, attitudes and suicide attempts and we must know how to handle the situation.

Suicide prevention, intervention, and post-intervention is one of the most important parts of chaplaincy to understand, if not the most important since a person is making an immediate decision of life or death that will alter not only their life but those that know and love them.

If a person confides in you that they're contemplating suicide then you need to ask them a difficult question that may seem unreasonable to ask; "Do you have a plan to carry it out?" By asking this question, you'll know if they are just trying to get attention or are they planning to end their life. If they have a plan, they'll give you details. It's at this moment that you need to get professional help, ASAP. You can do this by calling The Suicide and Crisis Lifeline at 988.

There are also apps you can put on your smartphone such as Suicide Safety Plan, and Suicide Prevention (by Health and Fitness) that will help you safely handle people in this mental and emotional crisis. The Suicide and Crisis Lifeline also have website you can navigate as well for more information. In 2020, an estimated 3.2 million people planned a suicide, 1.2 million attempted suicide and there were 45,979 people that actually ended their own life. In that year, 126 people took their own lives every day in the USA alone.

It is estimated that for every suicide, there are at least six survivors that are grieving their loss. Suicide is the second leading cause of death in young people ages 20-24 and it is the 10th leading cause of death in America. Suicide rates increase with age, and it has no boundaries, it affects all ethnic groups, ages, genders, or occupations. It affects the rich, the poor and everyone in between.

How do we prevent suicide? By listening and talking. Listen for red flags when you're talking with people. Unfortunately, some will never give a sign so openly discuss it, bring the subject to the forefront as the Lord leads and watch for clues.

There is so much to learn about suicide that it can't be discussed quickly. There is a lot of suicide among first responders, however, it's not just first responders who give up. People take their own lives through substance abuse as well. Statistics say nearly everyone, at some point in their life, thinks about suicide. Most everyone decides to live because they realize that the crisis that they are experiencing is temporary, but death is not.

Chaplains help people understand that Jesus is their hope. Even during an overwhelming crisis, if one will listen to Him, they won't end the valuable life God has given them. Unfortunately, there are many people who still don't know Jesus so we must be intentionally sharing His love.

What do we need to say, and how do we say it? Remain calm during these critical conversations. Never sound shocked, turned off, or make empty promises. Never leave the person alone or keep it a secret. These are the essential things we need to understand as a chaplain who is helping someone to make a decision to live, when everything in them is telling them to die.

Ask simple, straightforward questions, one at a time. Keep the questions simple, clear, and focused. Use closed-end questions that can only be answered with yes or no. Refrain from being assertive; give the person time to think through the answer. Don't try to prevent the expression of emotions such as crying. Give hope without giving false reassurance. Provide Scripture and any positive information or thoughts about the troubling situation they may be facing. Even if you can't fix it, simply being present, listening, and empathizing will be incredibly helpful and strengthening to the person in this mental crisis. I heard a pastor say to someone thinking about suicide one time, "God's not finished writing your story", and that stopped the suicide attempt. That man is living a wonderful life, married with children, and serving the Lord.

Can they be helped? *"The Lord is close to the brokenhearted; he rescues those whose spirits are crushed. The righteous person faces many troubles, but the Lord comes to the rescue each time." Psalms 34:18-19 NLT*

One of the questions you'll be asked is, "If my loved one committed suicide are they going to hell?" One answer would be: one can be mentally or emotionally ill just like one can be ill in their physical body. An illness does not send you to hell. The only decision that will keep you out of Heaven is a decision you made on earth to reject God's Son Jesus.

Are you called to save lives? Absolutely.

CHAPTER 5
GRIEF CHAPLAINS

A Grief Chaplain often works for a hospice organization and assists patients in their journey from life to death, as well as provide grief support for loved ones. Their ultimate goal is to help those in their care find peace and comfort during this transitional time at the end of their lives. For some, it is a difficult passage. For those that know the Lord, it's glorious.

Often times a chaplain, or even a friend, will be at a loss for words to say to the person dying and their loved ones. Especially if you're helping them transition from life to death during, or after, a crisis. Because of this I received the following words of wisdom from Chaplain Scott, whom I served with during a Foursquare Disaster Relief in Chico, California, after the Paradise Fire.

The best things to say to someone grieving:
1. I am so sorry for your loss.
2. I wish I had the right words; just know I care.
3. I don't know how you feel, but I am here to help in any way I can.
4. You and your loved one will be in my thoughts and prayers.
5. My favorite memory of your loved one is…
6. I am always just a phone call away.
7. Give a hug instead of saying anything.
8. We all need help at times like this; I am here for you.
9. I am usually up early (or late) if you need anything.
10. Saying nothing, just be present with the person.

The worst things to say to someone in grief:
1. At least she lived a long life; many people die young.
2. He is in a better place.
3. She brought this on herself.

4. There is a reason for everything.
5. Aren't you over him yet? He's been dead a long time.
6. You can still have another child.
7. She was such a good person that God wanted her to be with Him.
8. I know how you feel.
9. She did what she came to do, it was her time to go.
10. Be strong.

A person might just need a shoulder to cry on and sometimes it's just better not to say anything at all. That's why we need to pray continuously, under our breath, as we're listening to what the Lord might give you to encourage this person, or their family.

When asked 'why did this happen?', you may not always know the answer. Be truthful and tell them you don't know. Allow Holy Spirit to speak through His Word, but remember, sometimes people are hurting so much they have difficulty comprehending what's being said. Be there with love and empathy, because that's what a chaplain has to give, agape, the Godkind of love.

My pastors of many years, Tim and Barbara Odom, shared with me their story of helping a young, born-again woman transition from earth to Heaven. This is them, telling the story:

This young lady, who was a member of our church, had been suffering with cancer for many years and the hospital called us in for her final hours. We entered the room and asked her mom if she wanted to fight for her healing or if she wanted to go home to be with the Lord. Her mother answered, "she said she wants to go home to be with the Lord". So, I (Barbara) said, "lets help her". I began singing worship songs as I raised her pale hands from the white hospital sheets. I often stroked the hair from her face and saw a smile as we sang familiar songs to the Lord. The medical machines began to buzz, and her heart stopped beating. Pastor Tim said to her mom, "angels are in this room and their taking her home". The presence of angels was so tangible at that very moment that I wondered what she saw that I could not see.

Soon after the medical staff left the room her father entered and knelt beside the bed to weep loudly over his daughter. By this time, we had taken a seat in the room and could feel how much her parents loved her. Because we have two daughters of our own, we could empathize with them, and tears began to roll down both of our faces.

When they were finished with the initial grieving we stood and hugged their necks as we gave thanks to the Lord for the life He had given them to share, for such a short time. We sat in the room as the staff began to prepare her body for transport and her parents began to share moments that they had recently had with her as she prepared them for the choice she had made.

I'm sure that this young woman has never regrated the choice she had made to walk the streets of gold as she saw Jesus Himself. The One Whom she had spent much time talking to and reading His love letters to herself, aka: the Bible.

I know for us, it's a memorable highlight of our pastoral ministry. Ushering one of our church members, our friend, our sister in the Lord, into the very presence of God. Thank you for listening to how we tend to and care for the sheep God has entrusted to us.

This story you just read is one of many. This is what Pastors and Grief Chaplains do to serve people.

Are you called to be a Grief Chaplain?

CHAPTER 6
HOSPICE CHAPLAINS

A hospice chaplain works through a skilled professional care group. The experienced care is now directed to the patient's physical or psychological needs. However, the chaplain will help with the spiritual care. The hospice chaplain, with the team, will help with the patients' spiritual and emotional needs during the end-of-life process.

One of the important ministries of a hospice chaplain is that a patient should never die alone. You work with a team, and as the chaplain you build a relationship with the patient to be the go-between with their end-of-life journey. You are there to help them with their emotions such as anger, depression, and guilt. Help them understand they had a purpose and value here on earth. We are here to help guide the patient to a place of spiritual health by hopefully being able to lead them to Jesus and helping them see the value of their life and their positive impact.

This is going to be a challenging time for any chaplain. To be with somebody during their last days, week after week is not an easy thing. Yes, all chaplains can do this however God has gifted certain chaplains with a heart for hospice patients. It can be very emotional, more so than other areas. That's because most other areas are a short time, and helping at the end of life can be much longer and will can be emotional as you develop relationship with the patient and their family.

We must be careful that we don't overstep a line because the chaplain is not there to convert a patient into their religion, however as Christians we know that the way to the Father is through His Son, Jesus. And if given the opportunity, help them meet Jesus so in the next step they'll see Him face to face.

If the patient is not a Christian and does not want to hear about Jesus then do what you can to help them on a journey to discover meaning for their life here on earth, if at all possible. Regardless of the religion, creed, or culture a chaplain's purpose is to provide a patient with compassion, spiritual support, and spiritual advice.

The chaplain will also be dealing with the distress of the family. Helping the family to cope with these difficult emotions that they will be going through. Giving spiritual advice allows them to express their fears and voice their concerns during these difficult emotional times. Help the patient's caregiver with the painful process of losing a loved one. If you know for a fact that this person confessed Jesus as their Lord and Savior, you can confirm to the family that they have entered eternal life. If you don't know then walk very carefully in what you say and encourage the family with how much that person loved them.

The chaplain will encourage positive communication between the patient and their caregivers. The hospice chaplain will help caregivers stay informed and, more importantly, face these challenging times ahead.

The hospice chaplain becomes a trusted source of information and advice within the family unit of a terminally ill patient is dying. Over time a chaplain builds trust and a positive rapport with the family and would also obtain unique insight concerning what the family may need emotionally and spiritually.

Also, as hospice chaplains, we need to understand the different cultures and religions towards the needs of the patient. I know it's God's will that everybody to be saved and accept Jesus Christ into their life. However, during this progression, you may be ministering to a patient and their family with their different beliefs from your own. And after the patient is gone you will be ministering bereavement care to the family. Let them see the love of God.

Are you called to be a Hospice Chaplain?

CHAPTER 7
HEALTHCARE AND
HOSPITAL CHAPLAINS

Healthcare chaplaincy has been well documented from the early twentieth century. When hospitals were first established, they were usually an extension of a religious group that provided care. Later, hospitals began to care for people of many faiths. In doing so, multifaith needs were identified. When physicians recognized the advantage of providing spiritual care in addition to medical care, healthcare chaplaincy was born. Today many healthcare chaplains in the United States are trained in theology, psychosocial development, ethics, and a variety of other disciplines through seminaries, supervised clinical training, and other highly specialized forms of learning.

Because these on-call and part-time positions usually require a minimum of just one CPE (Clinical Pastoral Education) unit which is 400 hours of clinical training, they are open to local clergy. This includes individuals that represent various denominations such as Protestant Christian Pastors, Roman Catholic Priests, Jewish Rabbis, Islamic Imams, and more.

PRN (Pro-Re-Nata meaning as necessary) chaplaincy is also well suited for fully trained and certified chaplains who desire flexibility, or retirees wanting to continue ministering part-time.

Staff Chaplain: this position in a hospital setting typically requires a theological seminary education, ordination, and endorsement from the denomination that they are licensed with. There is no age or specific physical fitness requirement, but most institutions will require a minimum of four CPE units (1,600 hours) or a one-year residency. Another common requirement is that staff chaplains be board certified under the auspices of the Association of Professional Chaplains (APC).

Healthcare chaplaincy is conducted in a diverse and pluralistic setting where the patient did not go to the institution with the specific need or intent for spiritual care. The patient is a captive audience, often unable to leave his or her bed and vulnerable due to the hospitalization circumstances. Therefore, a chaplain making a "cold call" (an unrequested visit) must be especially sensitive to the needs and wishes of the patient as they relate to a ministry of spiritual care. Chaplains honor the "free exercise" clause of the first amendment by refraining from "evangelizing" and guarding against anyone else who might seek to proselytize or take unfair advantage of a patient in a vulnerable situation.

Healthcare Chaplains provide spiritual care through the critical ministries of presence, listening, and dialogue with patients, family, and other staff. They help redefine critical issues and sort out misunderstandings. Through their participation in the mutual journey, chaplains help patients, family, and staff re-evaluate values and beliefs that give meaning to life and relationships. As chaplains facilitate listening, they help all parties involved understand, integrate, and respond to the transcendent, even (and especially) in times of uncertainty, suffering, and pain.

Several people that are in the medical field go into global missions serving those with medical needs. Although the chaplain is not in the medical field team-leaders often need chaplains to go with the teams and serve the hurting as well as the team members. The chaplain is invited to pray with the staff that is giving the medical services and then be available to pray with the patients before and after the medical care. On these missions trips they also need help with paperwork; and you don't have to be a professional nurse or doctor to do that.

A chaplain may give God's word through scripture or prayer, but you may also be the one to give practical information that a chaplain shares with patients who lack knowledge or information. As a person that represents

Christ, the Healer, the chaplain often provides necessary information about how to accomplish a task, what the possible options are, who the potential resources are, or where help is available. Many people feel stronger and more able to cope with the circumstances of life when they have the information they need to deal with the situation.

How do you know how to serve best? You pray on the way to the hospital or spend time in prayer at home, and Holy Spirit will lead you. Then you make yourself available to those in charge.

Are you called to be a Healthcare Chaplain?

CHAPTER 8
COMMUNITY CHAPLAINS

Community Pastors, Priests and Rabbis usually minister to people with similar religious beliefs and who share many common cultural identities such as language, geographic location, socio-economic status, ethnic identity, education, age or any variation of a sub-culture.

On the other hand, chaplains typically minister to a people of many different religious beliefs, or no religious beliefs at all. These people represent many different cultural identities including age, ethnicity, gender, sport, education, profession, and political persuasion.

A congregation or ecclesiastical body gives community clergy authority, where-as chaplains are an allocated power by the institution that employs them and the clerical body that endorses them. Community clergy typically minister in a house of worship while the chaplain usually ministers in the marketplaces not traditionally considered "religious."

Across most religious lines, the community's spiritual leader is considered first to be a "minister," who officiates over the pastoral duties of the faith community. Likewise, the chaplain provides the religious functions people expect from the clergy of a local congregation. Often performing ministry without the physical structure of a church, synagogue, temple, or mosque, the chaplain may provide these religious functions in seemingly unusual places, i.e., offices, parks, beaches, disaster sites, homes, or public buildings. But to people who have never experienced "traditional" church, these locations will seem appropriate for the ministry provided.

Chaplains are often called upon to provide rites and rituals that are pertinent to Catholicism and some traditional denominational churches. These may include the celebration of marriages, baptisms, reading of last rights, infant dedications, christenings, and baptisms, as well as communion.

Some Chaplains even lead weekly worship services at different businesses, hospitals, and community gatherings. They may officiate at funerals, memorial services, and wakes. Depending upon the chaplain's ministry setting, other more atypical rites and rituals may be employed. The hospital chaplain may perform a "Blessing of the Hands", or as those in the Christian faith know it, "praying over the hands/person, for healthcare workers who attend to patients.

Upon hearing of a trucking fatality, the Truck-stop Chaplain may hold a memorial service over meatloaf and lemon pie. The Race-car Chaplain may pray over the team in the pits as crowds wait for the signal to "start your engines." The Disaster-Relief Chaplain may provide memorial services in the rubble of a building or home. These various places are often unique and characterized by the distinctive nature of each ministry.

When people are not church members, or regular attendees of any particular faith community, the chaplain may perform wedding ceremonies. These weddings may be conducted in rented facilities that often differ from the chaplain's place of worship. Many chaplains perform weddings as a regular part of their ministry. They also participate in graduations, banquets, buffets, dedications, programs, buildings, equipment, and other celebratory ceremonies. Law Enforcement Chaplains may wear agency uniforms and serve during the graduation ceremony of a police academy by leading the graduating officers in prayer or benediction.

Chaplains also assume the role of a representative of their faith and beliefs. Although techniques and methods vary among denominations or religions, others will have a view into the church that the chaplain represents. As religious pluralists, chaplains do not initiate a spiritual or evangelistic conversation, but by their character and actions, and their presence, they begin the relationship that might open the doors for sharing the Gospel. Because Americans enjoy the right to free exercise of religion, proselytizing (intentionally trying to convert someone to one's personal religious faith or belief system) is unadvised. Instead, chaplains find common ground for building relationships that build trust and encourage discovery of Truth.

Being a religious pluralist is not abandoning one's faith. But it does require strength and wisdom for the chaplain to be faithful to their faith and beliefs while being respectful of people whose faith traditions and practices differ from their own.

Are you called to be a Community Chaplain?

CHAPTER 9
CORPORATE CHAPLAIN

A corporate chaplain will serve at a business or a corporation. The chaplain might be an employee of that company and asked to work as a chaplain as needed for the ones who need to talk with a spiritual caregiver.

The chaplain is often called upon as a counselor for employees, clients, employers, and institutions. While providing counsel is helpful, the chaplain must clearly understand the difference between being a pastoral (or spiritual/Biblical) counselor and being a counselor in the therapeutic or clinical sense. Some Chaplains are exceptionally gifted or trained in counseling, however if they are not a licensed therapist, they must make it known that they give Biblical advice.

Counseling in chaplaincy is distinctive in that spirituality and God-consciousness is the basis for discussion and intervention. The reality of God within the relationship of counselor and counselee encourages reflections about faith, morality, sin, justice, mercy, and grace. The spiritual nature of a chaplain counseling enables clients and employers to consider issues confidentially from a personal perspective regardless of what is "politically correct."

The chaplain who offers counsel from a spiritual perspective must remain neutral to political issues. Yet, the chaplain must be faithful to the teachings and guidelines of their faith tradition. As ministers we must be dedicated to giving the truth of the Word of God.

The ministry of care must arise from a servant's heart, the heart of humility, compassion, and respect. The servant leader ministers so that the recipient experiences the Lord giving them an increase in well-being, feels less stressed, is more able to cope with the circumstances, and identifies possibilities for the future. The servant leader ministers to everyone with the same humble attitude. Everyone receives the same special attention and care. The chaplain who expects special treatment or recognition because of their status, education, title, or connections will be sadly disappointed when it is not forthcoming.

That's why we can work well in the workplace. A chaplain's ministry has often been called the "ministry of presence." Their presence is both physical and emotional. First, the chaplain consciously chooses to be physically present with the person. Second, the chaplain is emotionally current with the person through empathetic listening. Through his presence, the chaplain builds a relationship that comforts those who feel alone in their suffering or despair.

The 'ministry of presence' often looks like standing around the water cooler, circulating among the people, sitting quietly with someone, or having a cup of coffee in the lunchroom. 'Presence' may seem insignificant, but presence is the grace gift that chaplains bring to the human encounter. It is being available despite other commitments. It is being physically present even when the surroundings seem threatening. It is being emotionally present, although the anger or fear is uncomfortable. 'Presence' is the grace gift that accepts the person who seems or feels unacceptable.

Are you called to be a Corporate Chaplain?

CHAPTER 10
CONTINUING CARE RETIREMENT
COMMUNITY CHAPLAINS

Convalescent homes, aka: Nursing Homes is now often called a CCRC or Continuing Care Retirement Community where senior apartments, assisted living and nursing homes are all under the same roof, or on the same campus.

One of my most enjoyable assignments from the Lord was serving as a chaplain at a convalescent home. I learned to always pray on the way. Because I believe in praying in tongues I would pray in the spirit, and I would also pray in my understanding. Holy Spirit would give me insight into what He wanted me to say and He always knows the perfect will of God for the person I'm about to meet with.

Remember, this isn't all about us; it's all about Jesus, He's in us. All the praise and the glory should go to our Lord because we are nothing without Him. We are just a vessel being used by Him.

"Go ye therefore, and teach all nations, baptizing them in the name of the Father, and of the Son, and the Holy Ghost: Teaching them to observe all things whatsoever I have commanded you: and, lo, I am with you always, even unto the end of the world. Amen." Matthew 28:19-20

You don't just go and get people to repeat a prayer to get them to understand. As a chaplain, you're also a disciple maker. So, teach what the Lord has taught you. Yes, we want everybody to give their heart to the Lord because we don't want anyone to miss Heaven. Most of the time, there's a service once a week in the convalescent homes and that's also a good time to teach. But you can be a disciple-maker with just one person at a time.

If you make a disciple, they in turn will make disciples. Since you don't have the ability to talk with everyone, we can watch the multiplication the Lord does through people.

Pray for the sick and watch them recover as Jesus heals

them. Help people understand that Jesus has life for them today, as well as eternal life.

It's nice when you can lead them to Jesus, and they come to a service at the convalescent home. You can teach more people when you meet as a group, and often they receive more understanding when in a group because they help each other. Never be pushy. You might get kicked out of the convalescent home and not have an opportunity to return.

"For I know the thoughts that I think toward you, saith the Lord, thoughts of peace, and not of evil, to give you an expected end." Jeremiah 29:11

He gives us an expected end. The end of our life can be great. *"So as your days are, your strength will be". Deuteronomy 33:25.* If you live to be 120, Jesus can keep you strong and healthy. Jesus has provided us with peace, victory, joy, and purpose all the way to the end.

Please understand that working as a chaplain, you can work with other church organizations simultaneously. Does it mean you stop believing in your own faith's tenants? No, but we all believe in God the Father, Jesus Christ, and the Holy Spirit? It's excellent to learn to work with everyone to know our differences because the people you will be talking to at the convalescent homes will also be of various denominations.

For example, we might hold a church service for the residents during the week. When you provide a sermon, you'll preach one that fits all Christian denominations. And all you must do is use the Bible and preach the Word. Yes, there are spiritual gifts that God wants us to have, but not all understand that quite the same. The service time must be kept short because people need their sleep. And they love to sing, and if you can provide a little music with the service, they really enjoy it. Someone in the group might know how to play guitar, or they might have a keyboard, and someone knows how to play it. However, in the ministry I've been in, we don't have any of that, so I just use the music from my smartphone's playlist. I have a small Bluetooth speaker and

I choose older-generation gospel music that they probably remember. I love the new music, but the elderly love the old gospel music, they are usually not enthusiastic about the new contemporary Christian music.

Are you called to be a CCRC Chaplain?

CHAPTER 11
CRUISE SHIP, AIRPORT &
MOTORCYCLE CHAPLAINS

CRUISE SHIP CHAPLAINS

When praying about being a cruise ship chaplain ask the Lord if this is something He wants you to do for either a short trip or an extended ministry for months at sea. After all; *"We can make our plans, but the Lord determines our steps." Proverbs 16:9 NLT*

Another good scripture to know on a ship is; *"Thou hast enlarged my steps under me that my feet did not slip." Psalms 18:36*

One of the last things you might expect to see when you walk into a bar or a restaurant on a cruise ship is a priest, rabbi, minister, or chaplain…but they're there.

The cruise ship chaplain is classified as an entertainer and does not get paid; however, the ship will provide an accessible cabin. Even though you were titles as an entertainer, the administrators are expecting something else from a chaplain. The title is just a classification, not an identification.

Cruise ships have hired chaplains on board to give pastoral care to the crew. Large ships usually have around 1,000 crew members. Subsequently, they understand that they expect a lot of work from the crew and the crew needs spiritual care, or at least someone to listen. The crew is away from family members for months, they miss birthdays and anniversaries, and there are often great temptations one faces while away for so long.

They're able to get comfort in being able to speak to someone they can trust, and chaplains give comfort.

As a chaplain, you can go behind the scenes, anywhere on the ship where people work. And you are very much welcomed by the crewmembers in all the working areas, because they enjoy seeing you throughout their day.

The cruise chaplain will hold worship services, usually in

one of the restaurants or down below in the crew mess hall. Because of the unknown hours that many crew work, this worship service might be late at night, or early hours of the morning. The chaplain will also be offering a worship service for the guests on board and you will serve communion with the guests, and ship's crew, during your Sunday services.

Even though cruise lines have no obligation to provide religious services, border ships may choose to do so to help accommodate the faiths of their passengers. Thus, you might be the one God has sent to reach that one person with the Good News of Jesus, whether it be a crewmember or a passenger.

Are you called to be a Cruise Ship Chaplain?

AIRPORT CHAPLAINS

Another type of community chaplain is the chaplain at airports. Back in the 1950s, the country's first airport chapel was intended for staff rather than passengers and was established by Catholic leaders. The first one in the U.S. was "Our Lady of the Airways" and was built by Boston Archbishop Richard J. Cushing at Logan airport in 1951. Since then, other chapels have been built for all denominations and the traveling public now uses them, if they so choose. By 2020 there were 18 airports in the USA with chapels.

At various airports, there are different rules on the space of the chapels. They do not have Christian, Jewish, Muslim, Hindu, Buddhist, or other religious symbols. Mostly they are lined with plants or connected chairs in small areas. They set it up for the meditation and prayer of weary travelers. However, it is said that many of these facilities offer various worship services for different faith traditions.

Are you called to be an Airport Chaplain?

MOTORCYCLE CHAPLAINS

These chaplains are typically nondenominational because they are dealing with diverse groups of people. They typically volunteer and most of these chaplain's ride motorcycles. Subsequently, this chaplaincy is very specialized.

They participate in the motorcycle ministry that is on the rise. There are more than 100 national biker ministry organizations. Most have advanced chaplaincy training as biker chaplains. I'm not a biker chaplain, however I could pray for groups of bikers if I come across a unit. I welcome the opportunity to pray if I'm at a restaurant, hotel, or park.

Some biker chaplains I have talked to started as a rebel. They met Jesus and now they want to reach other bikers for the kingdom because they understand that life.

When you see a biker chaplain it's not who they were that matters, it's who they are now that they are in Christ.

Bikers are a very close-knit group. When they get saved, it's just like the rest of us, their minds must be renewed to the Word of God. That's where chaplains can help. Sometimes the chaplain will need to give Biblical encouragement when bikers express anger, or they might be needed for premarital counseling and perform weddings and funerals. These are the chaplains that are ministering to people that won't often walk into a church for one reason or another.

Chaplains will lead Bible studies and prayer groups. They'll baptize new believers and pray with bikers that have lost loved ones. They will love and accept the biker, as is.

Are you called to be a Motorcycle Chaplain?

CHAPTER 12
EMERGENCY SERVICE AND FIRE DEPARTMENT CHAPLAIN

The first thing I have to say is that it's so important to pray before you get to the emergency room or talk to anyone in the fire department about a crisis.

First responders often struggle with PTSD, because they face emergencies, deaths, and tragedies every day and we must be prepared to help the ones that are dealing with these tragedies. Sometimes you might think "how did I know to say that?", and it seems to be right on. It's because the Holy Spirit was ministering through you. Also, be very aware that there is an enemy, Satan, and he will try to confuse you so don't yield to him, rather resist him and he will flee.

Often times smells and sounds can set PTSD off. Most of the time you may not feel any different than normal, however a sound or smell can bring back memories and flashbacks and that could cause a reaction. According to a 2015 national survey of over 4000 police officers, paramedics, EMT's, and Fire-fighters, emergency workers are ten times more likely to attempt suicide than the average person experiencing PTSD. Roughly 6% of first responders surveyed have tried to commit suicide. So be compassionate with first responders. They've seen more than you would ever want to see.

With PTSD, one can be plagued by anger, disbelief, sadness, flashbacks, and can often withdraw from everyone. A person may be tempted to drink, abuse drugs or give in to any other addictions. One might start to have nightmares and fears of everything around them and often their marriages and families fall apart. It's because of the effects of PTSD.

When talking with someone experiencing these things you must remember listen and not do all the talking. Let the victim of PTSD talk. Then provide help where needed and pray with them. Some people don't understand how important it is to pray but to the individual going through this, they need someone that cares enough to pray.

A lot of first responders don't want to admit that they need help with mental and/or emotional help. They might fear negative repercussions at work, or among their peers for seeking help. But as a chaplain, recognize these areas in individuals and give them the encouragement that is so needed. If professional help, such as counseling is needed, please encourage them to avail themselves to it.

The fire department doesn't just fight fires. They have paramedics and EMT's that are also saving lives. Many times, they're saving lives in dangerous situations in large cities, such as Chicago, New York, Los Angeles, etc. They could be shot themselves, and sometimes they are. This kind of danger is always present, and it can spark effects of PTSD in our first responders.

The first responders can run on very little sleep during a long shift and as a first responder, they can't have a melt down when they have a victim in front of them. And as a chaplain, don't get in the way during a disaster, but be there to help the first responder through the traumatic events that keep happening throughout the months and years.

As a chaplain, you might be visiting a retired first responder. PTSD doesn't automatically leave one's mind just because they're retired. The flashbacks of the lives lost when they were trying to save them will sometimes affect them for years to come. Visit with them, listen to them, and pray with them because they are sometimes forgotten heroes.

Are you called to be an Emergency Service Chaplain?

CHAPTER 13
LAW ENFORCEMENT AGENCY
CHAPLAINS

The first thing you need to know is that before you can minister to Law Enforcement Officers you must gain their trust, and that comes with relationship. Just showing up and being there in case someone needs you to listen to them or pray with them is important. As always, it's important to talk to the Lord in your heart before you talk. The work they do can affect them mentally, physically, and relationally. Many law enforcement officers experience PTSD to some degree and some believe their career would be in jeopardy if they disclosed their symptoms of PTSD. So it might be difficult to build trust, but here are a few scriptures that could help minister to an officer:

"Blessed are the peacemakers: for they shall be called the children of God." Matthew 5:9 KJV

"The wicked flee when no man pursues: but the righteous are bold as a lion." Proverbs 28:1

"Love worketh no ill to his neighbor: therefore, love is fulfilling the law." Romans 13:10

I often pray this for our officers: "Father God, we thank You for watching over our police officers, for leading them in their decisions and for protecting them. Continue to guide them as they keep us safe both day and night. Hold them firmly in your care should danger come their way. Give them strength and courage as they serve till their duty has ended. In Jesus' name, amen."

Police officers face a plethora of difficult scenes daily and could use someone to talk to or at least someone to listen and pray for them. They see people that have been severely injured, or killed, in unimaginable accidents and crisis. They see families torn apart by domestic violence, and even murder. Often officers, that are also parents, are affected by children that have been hurt or traumatized because they have children of their own and they can empathize.   Often, they see body parts that have been severed, they witness murders, and many times they themselves are almost killed, or see a fellow-officer killed, while serving us in the line of duty. Most of the time our officers are the ones on the scene before any other first responders and they see the worst of the worst.

There are many states, in the U.S., that provide resources for our first responders with effects of PTSD. However, there are some first responders that still feel uncomfortable sharing the feelings their facing. So, as a chaplain, you must respect that they need someone to help but you also must be careful not to put them in jeopardy of their jobs, or relationships. In some places they are told to "suck it up" and "deal with it", but over time this takes a toll on a person mentally and emotionally effecting every relationship they have.

We all know that law enforcement officers are human beings. We all have emotions, and when we see tragedy after tragedy, it will affect us, everyone to a different degree.

This is why praying and letting the Holy Spirit lead you when you start to talk with them is so important. This is an important time to make sure you listen more than you talk.

There are classes through ICISF that will help you in helping others with critical incident stress. They have several classes and networking choose from and you can take these classes as your time allows, it's not necessary to take them all at the same time. You can find these resources by going to www.icidf.org.

I highly recommend the Pastoral Crisis Intervention course as a chaplain. It would help you know how to communicate with first responders because in a disaster, you will give advice to help people mentally, emotionally, spiritually, and theologically.

In one of the classes that I took we had a scenario that we were roleplaying. It was of a police officer that had no choice and had to shoot a man or be shot. I don't care how "macho" a person is those kinds of conditions mess with a person's head. Nobody wants to kill another human being, whether on purpose or not. However, there are times when a police officer has no choice. In this instance, the police officer walked away to be alone, even after he was told everything he did was correct. So, a chaplain enters the scene in this scenario.

The person I was role-playing with said to me "why aren't you talking? You need to be talking to me." I said I needed to listen to the Holy Spirit before I spoke in this instance. That particular person had never been in a disaster and probably doesn't understand that you need to take it slow and get the hurting person to talk, not do the talking yourself. People are hurting and we're there to help. According to Luke 4, part of our purpose is to bring "healing to the brokenhearted" just as Jesus did.

DR. MARILYN NEUBAUER'S STORY

Dr. Marilyn Neubauer, D.Th. shared a story with me and gave me permission to share it with you. She is a traveling itinerate minister and a police chaplain in Southern California. I first heard her share this story at Spirit Life Church, in Bullhead City, AZ many years ago, and it always stayed with me. Understand these things happen very fast when you make decisions to help people in dangerous situations while riding along in police cars. She begins:

I have been a Chaplain for almost 17 years. It's been an honor to serve my community in this capacity. I serve in several different areas most often I drive in police cars with the officers. As a chaplain my first duty is to be the officer's second pair of eyes. Sometimes it's difficult for them to be driving and looking for a victim or suspect on the street at the same time. Many times, I have spotted the person or seen something that needed their attention before they saw it. I've often heard the comment, "good eye chaplain".

One evening I was riding with a young officer who was a strong Christian. This is one of those situations where speaking about the Lord is just natural. I shared many things with him that he had never been taught. I emphasized that as a Christian, he has inside information that he didn't learn at the academy. That his job is dangerous, and he should learn to listen within his spirit. This was very new to him, but he thought it was awesome. I recognized he had a call of God upon his life, probably that of a pastor.

He was very interested in Bible school and wanted to know how I got into the ministry. I suggested that he not pack up and move away to attend a Bible school since he and his wife just had their first child, and he was only a few months out of the police academy. Instead, I suggested that he could take a Bible correspondence course. He liked that idea very much and I said I would bring him some information about such a course.

The following morning during my devotional time, I sensed the Lord was impressing upon me to NOT take the correspondence material to him that night. In the natural, I couldn't imagine why since it was a good thing to do. However, I knew not to question the Lord, but obey. I could always give it to him the following week.

Later that day while working in my office I noticed the time was 3 o'clock. I immediately thought, I need to get dressed and go to the police station to ride with this officer. At that very moment, I heard within my spirit, the Holy Spirit saying, "Remember, don't go today." "Oh, that's right, thank you for reminding me."

This was at 3 o'clock and at 5 o'clock this sweet, precious young police officer was shot and killed during a routine traffic stop. Even though I had the opportunity to share how to listen to the voice within, we don't learn overnight.

This was our first murder in 100 years. I was called into the station and asked how I would have handled that situation. I, like the officer, was very new as a chaplain, only a few months into my ministry with them.

When asked how I would have responded, I said, first I would call for backup. Second, since I don't use a weapon,

I would have gotten down on the floor of the car to get out of range. However, I already knew what I was about to be told had I had been there.

The Lieutenant said, "In that case, the car would have been your coffin." You see, the man that killed the officer was already a criminal and after shooting the officer, he stole the police car to use as his "get-away" and I would have been right there with him. I am sure this man would have had no mercy on me because my shirt sleeve said, "Chaplain". Only the Lord knew what was about to happen and he warned me through the Spirit.

I was very saddened that this officer was killed, but so thankful I knew the voice of the Lord and how to obey even when I could not see any reason why I could not have gone that night. John 16:13 tells us, *"However, when He, the Spirit of truth, has come, He will guide you into all truth; for He will not speak on His authority, but whatever He hears He will speak; and He will tell you things to come."*

The job of the Holy Spirit is to be our guide. His guidance will always protect and keep us safe. We must learn to listen and never let logic overrule us.

Are you called to be a Law Enforcement Chaplain?

CHAPTER 14
MILITARY CHAPLAINS

Perhaps the most documented history of chaplains is in the area of Military Chaplaincy. From ancient times, chaplains have served the military of the world. The Continental Congress recognized the need for professional chaplains and authorized salaries equal to regimental surgeons, thereby elevating chaplaincy to a professional status. Today, chaplains serve in all branches of the United States military as officers and professional caregivers.

Always pray before you talk to any military organization. Ask the Lord; "is this where you want me to serve?" Because this is a commitment to the Lord, but also the US Military and the rules are different from civilian life. You must do the following:

Step 1: Earn at least a bachelor's degree. The Army requires chaplains to have a bachelor's degree consisting of at least 120 credit hours and 72 semester hours in graduate work.
Step 3: Gain experience as a spiritual leader, either on a pastoral staff or in another area of chaplaincy.
Step 4: Meet military requirements from the particular branch of military you will be serving.
Step 5: Complete any training required for chaplains.

Chaplains are unique officers within their units. They receive the rank of a captain either upon entry or after they have been in active duty. Although they do hold rank and authority granted by the military, but they will never have command authority. Which means they will not be over a unit in a fighting capacity.

A military chaplain does not go through basic training. Instead, they attend a Chaplain Officer Basic Course (CHOBC), which is a 12-week course taught at Fort Jackson South Carolina. It provides you with instruction on the noncombat common core skills on a written and chaplaincy-specific training. All the branches have similar requirements.

Chaplains are in the military, but they do not fight in combat. However, chaplains may be deliberately or indiscriminately attacked if their retention by the enemy is required to provide for the most affluent needs of prisoners of war. Hopefully chaplains will not become POW's because they will not necessarily know the rules of war.

Chaplains go anywhere that the military goes. The chaplain's responsibilities include performing religious rights, conducting worship services, providing confidential counseling, and advising commanders on religious, spiritual, and moral matters.

Chaplains do not carry weapons unless it's necessary. As such they are not supposed to be targeted by the enemy. There are some U.S. chaplains that have received combat training to be better able to move with the troops. There have been chaplains that have died in work zones and during WWII the Army and the Marines lost more chaplains than they have ever lost in a war.

Many chaplains require an engaged couple to take premarital counseling before he/she will perform the marriage ceremony, just as most pastors do. Weddings are conducted for free by active or reserve chaplains. They cannot receive financial gain by accepting monetary donations for performing a wedding.

If you adhere to the Biblical teaching of the marriage of only one man and one woman, then you will need to disclose this before accepting a chaplaincy with the military.

From those that join our military 20% confess no religion, or they claim to be agnostic or atheist. Therefore, chaplains must be trained to minister not only to those from diverse religions but also those that claim no god. Across the branches of military there are more than 100 different faith groups that have chaplains that represent them. At least 93% of chaplains are representing Christianity, and at least 50% of those come from evangelical denominations.

There are some atheists that are trying to claim discrimination if they are not allowed to be a military chaplain. But I'm not sure how an atheist could serve those that believe in God, or why they would want to. After all, the Army's motto is 'For God and Country' so how could an atheist fulfill that motto if, by definition, they do not believe in God? Our chaplains' religious freedoms, and the religious freedoms of our men and women serving in our military are being threatened every day and their constitutional rights are being infringed on so please pray for our military chaplains and those making decisions.

A chaplain is there to comfort our military whether at home in the USA, or when they go off to war. The Chaplains have a long history of jumping into the foxholes with our men and women, fighting for our freedom.

During WWII there were four chaplains. Lieutenant George L. Fox, Methodist; Lieutenant Alexander D. Goode, Jewish; Lieutenant P. Washington, Roman Catholic; and Lieutenant Clark V. Poling, Dutch Reformed. These four chaplains spread out among the soldiers who were extremely frightened to help calm the soldiers and guide them toward safety. These four chaplains gave their lives for these men during wartime, and in doing so for your freedom, and mine. They were all given distinguished service crosses and purple hearts. They were absent in person to receive this honor but received a greater honor given to them as they entered Heaven. On their behalf, their families received a one-time-only post-mortem special medal for heroism. Although we lost some, these four chaplains helped to save a lot of men on that ship that day.

Are you called to serve our military?

CHAPTER 15
PRISON CHAPLAINS

Spiritual care for the incarcerated is as established as the institutions of incarceration themselves. This is particularly true in the Christian tradition, which has taken to heart the lessons of Matthew 25, visiting those in prison. Long before federal prisons were erected, city jails had visiting clergy who intentionally ministered to the needs of people who had been incarcerated.

Today correctional chaplains are professionals with specialized training, representing their faith communities. They serve in many federal, state, county, and local facilities.

There may be differences between the requirements for education and training to be a prison chaplain than any other kind of chaplain. The Federal Department of Corrections (FDC) requires chaplains to meet the requirements of age (less than 37 years old at the time of application), suitability (in employment, financial, and criminal history), and physical standards (pass drug tests and physical abilities test). There are in addition to the usual requirements of education (earned M.Div. or the equivalent), experience (one CPE unit plus one year of residency), religious credentials (ordination or comparable status), and finally, ecclesiastical endorsement for correctional chaplaincy.

Correctional chaplains are often required to have additional specialized training related to suicide intervention, the criminal justice system, restorative justice issues, diversity within the correctional institution, and victimology. Prison chaplains are also well-trained in substance abuse counseling and conflict resolution.

The requirements for volunteer correctional chaplains vary from one facility to another. In most cases, ordination and a graduate theological education are not necessarily required. However, volunteer Chaplains will certainly be required to submit to security and credit checks. They must also provide references from their denominational leader and participate in the institution's orientation and training programs. Generally, volunteer correctional chaplains must be at least twenty-one years of age.

Correctional chaplains provide spiritual care to those who are imprisoned and separated from their family and friends and from society in general. These chaplains also provide spiritual care to the institutional staff and the family members of staff and inmates, as requested.

Correctional chaplains provide the ministry of presence as they enter the world of locked doors, barbed-wire fences, armed guards, and painful solitude. They enter the suffering of defeated people who live with anger, depression, loneliness, hostility, and even despair. They penetrate the darkness of prisons while providing for the free exercise of religion for all inmates.

Before entering the prison, make sure you pray because you are going to experience some of the most disturbed people who might have never known the Lord, or even heard of Him. Then there will be others that knew the Lord at one time in their life and they just fell into temptation, sinned, and got caught.

It has been in my heart to become a prison chaplain one day. My friend, Chaplain Karen Tavasci, told me the visits and Bible Studies need to be short because you don't have much time with anyone at one given visit. Praying for the prisoner will be part of your visit, however, you're not allowed to touch a prisoner. There may be chaos outside of the room in which you are meeting with the man or woman you came to minister to so stay focused. You're there for the one person, or one group that has invited you into their lives to bring them Good News.

Inmates suffer the same disappointments, hurts, and grief that others face on the outside. They experience separation, broken relationships, betrayal, demotions, disappointments, deaths, deteriorating self-esteem, physical illness or disease, emotional turmoil, or distractions, financial or economic hardships, and spiritual crises. The difference between inmates and the average citizen is that inmates experience these things in complete isolation, separated from loved ones and support systems. The very nature of their circumstances makes them more vulnerable to emotional and spiritual distress.

Correctional chaplain's function in all the same roles as a chaplain serving other areas. As administrators, they manage worship services and advise on many issues surrounding faith practices, providing opportunities for all prisoners to practice their faith while honoring the right of others to practice no faith, if they so choose.

Frequently, administration in this setting also requires coordinating and managing a pool of volunteers who minister to inmates. This may include recruitment, training, supervision, and evaluating volunteers from many faith communities. As religious pluralists, correctional chaplains must encourage the participation of many religious traditions to meet the needs of the inmates.

Correctional chaplains are well known for their role as pastors and spiritual caregivers. In prison, this care may take the very practical form of assisting with letter writing, reading through difficult letters or documents, visiting families of the incarcerated, or sitting with a prisoner who is awaiting surgery, trial, parole hearings, or even death.

As educators, correctional chaplains are often called upon to teach classes or facilitate support groups. They may teach seminars on grief recovery, stress management, anger management, life skills, or conflict resolution. They teach inmates how to cope with their circumstances and prepare for employment. They also find resources for inmates to receive training or education for new jobs or vocations.

In many cases, chaplains are also educators for the institution, teaching the staff and administrators to have some of the same skills. In the correctional setting, the chaplain's role as the minister may seem less critical, but many prison chaplains also have the opportunity to organize church services. They officiate at weddings and funerals and perform liturgical duties as required by their own denominations or faith traditions. They provide individual and corporate prayer for inmates and the institution.

Correctional chaplains are also crisis interventionists. They provide a calm presence in chaos. As inmates experience rejection for parole, divorce, or other crises that disrupt their emotional balance, chaplains are called upon to provide acute emotional support. They may engage in suicide intervention or assessment of referral needs. When there is a crisis in the correctional institution, the chaplain is often the reminder that God is present in the chaos.

Finally, correctional chaplains act as vital advocates for the inmates and liaisons between the institution and the community of faith, raising awareness about the needs of the incarcerated and their families. They advise community clergy on matters about prison ministry and promote an understanding of how to assist inmates as they make the transition into the community after being confined.

However, in their work with inmates and their families, correctional chaplains must be careful not to imply advocacy in terms of lawlessness, nor may they ever give legal, medical, or psychological advice.

Unique factors in the environment within the correctional institution breed many issues that intensify with the level of security of the institution. Jails, prisons, and penitentiaries all deal with inmates who succumb to peer pressure while confined. The pressure to conform to the attitude of "criminals" or "bad guys" is a coping mechanism for those who feel weak and vulnerable. The correctional chaplain is constantly dealing with inmates' fear of being perceived as weak and exposed because they have chosen to make a lifestyle change, abandoning a life of criminal activity.

Inmates also deal with issues of depersonalization and dehumanization. They fear breaches of confidentiality, prejudice, and discrimination. For some, fear is the natural outcome of the impending release, resettlement, or even execution. Correctional chaplains have the difficult task of building trust with inmates through personalizing their relationships, humanizing their circumstances, equalizing their perceived injustices, and fostering peace and reconciliation in circumstances of all forms of bias.

The environment of the correctional institution is often a microcosm of the greater world of crime outside the bars, guarded walls, and monitored rooms of the prison. Thus, prison chaplains need to understand the complicated nature of gangs, sexual assault, drugs, and crime. These are frequent issues inside prison walls and in the world beyond. Correctional institutions create acute vulnerability for chaplains. They are vulnerable to exploitation by experienced manipulators, to showing favoritism to those who demonstrate an interest in matters of faith, and to breaching confidentiality when questioned by those in authority or by those who seem casually interested. They are susceptible to stereotyping, personal prejudices and biases, and exhaustion from intense, long-term spiritual care.

I have a friend that shared with me a story from her uncle, who prior to his passing due to old age, was a Prison Chaplain that served on death row. Her uncle told her that he was the last person that a man would see before he was escorted to death. Her uncle was the one that would order this man's last meal and he would say the last words this man would hear, so the chaplain had to choose his words well. Those last words were about Jesus, and God's love for him. Most of the time these men would weep as they repented of their sin and would confess Jesus as their Lord. It's by God's grace that any of us deserve forgiveness and the same blood of Jesus that forgave us forgave these men too and will pardon anyone who sincerely repents.

The human worth and dignity of these individuals is confirmed by the chaplain because the chaplain is a picture of God's grace and mercy for all of mankind.

Are you called to be a Prison Chaplain?

CHAPTER 16
SOUP KITCHENS CHAPLAINS

"For I was hungry, and you gave me meat: I was thirsty, and you gave me drink; I was a stranger, and you took me in." Matthew 25:35

Soup kitchens are typically serving the homeless and they need chaplains to minister natural food to the people as well as spiritual food. Most soup kitchens will serve the homeless, serve the low income, those that might not have had enough money to buy groceries that week, and those that are simply one paycheck away from losing their housing. We have probably all fallen into one of these categories.

The number of people that either find themselves homeless or choose to be homeless is growing in our nation. Among them is a large percentage of people with addictions and mental disorders.

We wonder with the amount of job openings we see daily why this remains an issue. My personal opinion is that once a person gets on the street and yields to depression, rejection and hopelessness, they simply give up like so many others have done. But the chaplain at the soup kitchen can help restore hope through serving food and presenting Jesus, the answer to the myriad of questions they have.

The chaplain gives a word of hope from Scripture. We help people understand God loves them today, right now, right where they're at and He has a path that leads to peace and provision for them.

The Apostle Paul put it this way: *"When I am with those who are weak, I share their weakness, for I want to bring the weak to Christ. Yes, I try to find common ground with everyone, doing everything I can to save some." 1 Corinthians 9:22.*

Then Luke 1:37 says, *"For with God, nothing shall be impossible."* And the Prophet Isaiah in 35:3 says, *"With this news, strengthen those with tired hands, and encourage those with weak knees."*

We cannot heal the mentally ill or deliver one from addictions, but Jesus can. When talking with people make sure they can understand what you're saying, or how will they apply the truth to their circumstance?

Most people would not welcome the homeless into their homes for various reasons. However, people need to be shown the love of God, where they walk, live and sleep. That non-judgmental, uncompromised, never-ending love.

You are there to listen to people, to really listen. Allowing people to have the ability to share their hurt and pain. Sometimes you'll be able to help them solve their problems and sometimes you won't but listening and praying with people will always help.

As a chaplain we need to be able to tell the Gospel story and, why God sent His Son Jesus, and how that applies to them today. Jesus gave His life for others on the same day He gave His life for me. And then, He rose victoriously giving victory to us today. He did that for every human, no matter where they live, or what they've done.

Sadly, the facts are that there are very few soup kitchen chaplains because of the typical mental and emotional issues many homeless some struggle with. Other reasons are people might smell like they haven't bathed, because they haven't. They might have anger issues or be hiding from the law. But every person needs a spiritual encounter with Jesus.

The thing to remember is this, God knows each one by name, He loves them, and He's sending you to represent His love and acceptance. Are you called to be a chaplain to the homeless?

CHAPTER 17
SPORTS CHAPLAINS

The sports chaplain provides pastoral care for the sports community, including athletes, coaches, administrators, and their families. Various sports and cultures may adopt the practice of sports chaplaincy but under different titles. It could be a Sports Mentor, Life Coach, or Character Coach. Consequently, the practice of working as a Sports Chaplain is broad in scope but it brings prayer and encouragement and helps build their faith through the Word of God.

Sports chaplaincy began in Greece, 336 A.D. when chaplains performed ceremonial religious functions where elite sports athletes discussed their beliefs with the chaplains, in a private place.

Sports Chaplains consists of people from various denominations. Most commonly, the chaplains and/or ministers are full-time Christian workers however chaplaincy work is done typically without any financial compensation. The chaplain provides spiritual support and guidance to the players and can also emphasize and relate to some of the challenges the athletes face. Helping them to understand that even in sports, God is with them.

However, because there is no financial assistance, only a few chaplains travel with the teams. The teams that are part of the NFL hire chaplains that can serve them full time, even while traveling. When college or local teams play, they often have people that will donate funds in order to have a chaplain travel with them because the coaches know that their athletes need the spiritual support of a chaplain. The coaches can verify that the chaplains encourage their players through prayer and a word of encouragement from Scripture. Being away from home and families can be an added stress. So having a chaplain to talk with is extremely beneficial.

Even though some athletes are not believers, there are

many athletes that are Christians and understand that without Jesus, they can do nothing. There have been some who stood for what they believed and were ridiculed for doing so. I'm thankful for the athletes that don't back down from the truth.

Then there are some teams that do have a chaplain on their payroll. The average salary of a sports chaplain is $51,000 per year. Some chaplains are funded by Athletes in Action, a ministry founded in 1966 that focuses on the athletes and living out their relationship with Jesus. Athletes in Action also develop Bible study groups in High Schools, Colleges, and Universities across the USA.

A chaplain can also provide outside activities with the team members. Such as overseeing a Bible study with a group of athletes or their family members. He might also be providing pastoral care, baptisms, and weddings if the athletes do not have a local pastor.

To become a sports chaplain, you technically need a BA or MA in theology or divinity, and other required credentials from a recognized church or religious organization. Some denominations have training programs for clergy members to become sports chaplains. It doesn't matter the faith you practice but you must be able to provide non-denominational services when working with the teams.

Unfortunately, atheistic views have made it very difficult for ministers and chaplains to serve in public schools. Yet professional sports still accept our services. Christian coaches might have to be careful of what they say, but chaplains have more freedom.

From Little League to High School to College to the NFL, it's an honor to serve our athletes through prayer, encouragement, and the Word of God. Are you called to be a Sports Chaplain?

CHAPTER 18
CHAPLAINS AND CRISIS

A crisis or disaster intervention is one of the fastest-growing areas of chaplain specialization. Crisis Chaplains often serve multiple agencies and usually respond to the general community of victims during the crisis. Victims may include:

- Direct victims
- Innocent bystanders
- Rescue and relief workers
- First responders
- Perpetrators of crimes (e.g., the arsonist who starts the forest fire, the drunk driver who causes the multi-car fatality, or the terrorist who plants the bomb).

Crisis intervention is a short-term helping process. It is an acute intervention designed to stabilize and mitigate the crisis response. With this, there is Psychological First Aid known as PFA. It's a term used to denote one verification on a term of crisis intervention CISM system. PFA dates back to World War II but did not gain favor until 2005. The John Hopkins RAPID model of PFA is a popular model developed as a means of training first responders to enhance the community's search capacity from a public health and public safety perspective so, if you're a chaplain, you need to understand the requirements as you deploy to a disaster.

Whenever people experience an event that disrupts their emotional or psychological balance to the extent that their usual coping mechanisms fail, they are in crisis. They need urgent and acute psychological support. This support is called Crisis Intervention. The crisis may seem minor to some observers, but the personal perception of the crisis will determine the level of distress experienced by that individual.

A broken leg may seem like a rite of passage to a teenage

motorcyclist, but the same broken leg may be the end of a career for a professional athlete. Thus, Chaplains may provide crisis intervention for a vast array of situations, each one a crisis to the individual involved.

Several studies have indicated that following a terrorist event such as the Oklahoma City bombing in 1995, people near the disaster did not think they needed help and would not seek services, despite reporting significant emotional distress. (Meyer, 1991; Sprang, 2000). It's a standard thought, as with other disasters as well. Many survivors state that others need assistance far more than they themselves.

Our purpose is to represent Jesus to others. It could be during riots, violence, social discord, disaster, or terrorism. The appropriate training in crisis intervention and emergency mental health could provide much-needed support in community discord and a mass disaster. We don't offer assistance just for Christians, we provide for all. Which means we help people of different ethnicities, backgrounds, religious faiths and sometimes no faith at all. We will be there to help start their road to recovery and to help them emotionally and spiritually.

Pastoral crisis intervention is a term that represents the functional immigration of a psychological crisis intervention with pastoral care. Crisis intervention is best understood in the context of the term 'crisis'.

Pastoral care may be seen as providing spiritual or faith-oriented leadership. Pastoral care is typically provided by someone licensed or ordained in ministry. They have been commissioned to be a representative of a faith-oriented group or other organization to provide emotional support, religious education, worship, sacraments, community organization, decision-making, related activities, and spiritual support.

Some pastoral care will provide counseling. When a chaplain functions in providing pastoral care, they will be confronted with the challenges of an acute psychological or spiritual crisis. It can mean that they will serve in a house of worship, a hospital, a nursing home, and at the scene of an accident or disaster.

They might also serve at a funeral home or gravesite during a crisis. For those who rise to meet such challenges, a solid grounding in theology, spirituality, and pastoral care is only the beginning. They should also be trained and familiar with supportive resources, including psychological, psychiatric, and other resources.

There are five core components of crisis intervention.
1. Assessment and screening of a person or persons in a state of psychological crisis to provide and facilitate access to the most appropriate care.
2. Applicable psychological principles and practices to stabilize and, if possible, migrate acute stress.
3. If necessary, liaison and advocacy intervention to serve as a mediator or advocate for the person, or persons in distress.
4. Spiritual interventions are generally acceptable across most religious beliefs. Extraordinary crisis intervention may commonly consist of individual prayer, conjoint prayer, the ministry of presence, pastoral crisis intervention, and divine intervention.
5. Religious interventions would be based upon specific religious doctrine, belief, and scripture. Examples of religious intervention would be spiritual rituals of worship, sacraments, interpretation, insight, practices of confession, forgiveness, or death-related ways.

The crisis is when a violation of one's identity, worldview, and sense of trust and safety has occurred. The individual's physical health, life experience, and depth of relationship with God, could be altered due to the crisis so we must step in and truly care for the person in front of us.

When crisis occurs, I recommend you give people presence, let them speak, and let them get things off their chest. They may feel abandoned, but they are never abandoned by God. They may find it hard to pray, but as a chaplain, help them, pray for them. Give them hope because Jesus is the hope they're looking for. The chaplain will confirm that everything will turn around in due time. Even some of the best Christians with the most understanding can lose it during a crisis. There were three young men that faced a crisis. Here's what their reply was:

"Shadrach, Meshach, and Abednego replied, "O Nebuchadnezzar, we do not need to defend ourselves before you. If we are thrown into the blazing furnace, the God whom we serve can save us. He will rescue us from your power, Your Majesty. But even if He doesn't, we want to clarify to you, Your Majesty, that we will never serve your gods or worship the gold statue you have set up." Daniel 3:16-18 NLT

If crisis is taking place because a government is trying to get us to do something outside of God's instructions to us then we must be like Shadrach, Meshach and Abednego and say, "we will never serve other gods", and we will be rewarded.

There is a protocol for pastoral crisis intervention and guidelines. Here they are:

Pre-Crisis

1. Become familiar with the culture of the potential population for your crisis work.
2. Participate in and observe operations, incidences, and training sessions.
3. Develop a normative spiritual baseline or religious profile of the potential recipient population. (Know who you're serving).
4. Develop and cooperate with service and department protocols.
5. Carry a list of available resources with Local addresses and phone contact parameters for referral and follow-up.

Incident Specific

1. Respond and participate with pre-establish protocols.
2. Be prepared to act in symbolic and sacramental function.
3. Know those you're serving with and introduce yourself to them for identification purposes.
4. Assist in the triage with other leaders, such as ministers, priests, rabbis, and imams. Know your proper role in each emergency or disaster scene.
5. Remember, when working with emergency personnel, they are in operation demobilization. They need the presence of caring, comforting, guiding, and healing persons, not an official!

During Crisis Intervention

1. Integration is a prime function for the chaplain. We must be prepared emotionally for what we might experience.
2. Persons in crisis may be surprised at their feelings about values, beliefs, and God so they may experience shame or guilt. Create an accepting, supportive atmosphere.
3. Be prepared to protect the person from others who are reacting to the idea that God is powerless, useless, or dead.
4. People need to be heard and excepted and questions have yet to be answered.
5. Be attentive and aware of interference, resistance, or acceptance of your faith to their new belief arising out of the search after being involved in an overwhelming incident.

Post-crisis

1. Continue to be a listener.
2. Maintain open communication. Ask the person. who you're helping in crisis what they need, and what they don't need - then honor it.
3. Educate persons in crisis, and those around them, about the discomfort, and value, of the grief and despair they and others are experiencing.
4. Help persons in crisis engage and connect to resources and reliable referrals.
5. Be a companion along the journey. Give control to the person in crisis in the hope that a new possibility can fill the emptiness.

I remember my first deployment. My leaders assigned a very seasoned chaplain to go with me to the field. I wasn't very confident in myself to serve the first crisis victim they assigned me to. But all the victim needed was a shoulder to cry on, so I didn't need to say anything. In fact, my shoulder was just the right height for her to lay her head on as she wept. I'm thinking of that first day in the disaster area, and although I trained well enough one never thinks they're ready. So, I listened, learned, and followed the instructions of my seasoned lead chaplain.

The second-day, I was in the same area of deployment and a woman was so out of control that I was thinking "what I am going to say and what I am going to do?". I can only remember about 10% of what I said. I knew more than ever, I needed the Holy Spirit, and He was faithful. This woman was screaming and crying, and I was told she had been distressed for about a week. I remember I talked for a few minutes and then I listened. Whatever I said was ordered by the Lord because in the end, she stopped crying and had a smile on her face for the first time in a week. The part that I do remember saying is "you need to help your neighbors, and the neighbors will help you".

I believe that God sent help from Holy Spirit and gave her the word she needed to hear so she could move forward in her journey of healing and restoration.

Most of the time, a chaplain in these situations doesn't get to see that person a second time. That makes it more essential to understand the protocol and let the Holy Spirit lead you. Yes, your training is going to help. It is specialized training and that's why I highly recommend ICISF. But the best training is in the field where it's all happening. You will be with well experienced chaplains, and you'll walk away with experiential knowledge.

Because I'm with a Pentecostal disaster relief team, when we get together as a group we pray in the Spirit, and in our understanding, asking the Holy Spirit to come in and be with us during prayer before we even start our day. Then the lead chaplain gives us our assignments, our partners and what to expect.

When we return to base camp, we review our day with our leaders, assessing victories and obstacles alike. We're asked how we're doing emotionally, physically, and spiritually and what we want to do to cope with what we saw. Then we pray for each other. The more we debrief the more we begin to open up with one another and disclose what we're feeling about what we experienced. The sights, the sounds, the smells, and the precious people devastated.

On the field there is not one day the same when you're out on deployment. But the Lord is with you, and He's made His home in you. He'll help you navigate every change you encounter.

Not only do you have the Lord with you, but you are not alone in the natural either. You must have a co-chaplain with you. It is best if there is a male and female chaplain working together, but sometimes there's not enough people to go around. There are safety reasons for this, as well as the reasons of accusations that can be made of one gender or another. It's not imperative that a male chaplain minister to males and a female chaplain minister to females. It's whoever has the word of encouragement, whoever feels led to pray.

Some disasters have a designated location for spiritual care and mental health assistance, and they are waiting for people in need to reach out. It's imperative that they are sensitive to those passing by so that they might help those that are helping others.

After the crisis has subsided it's important to gather survivors and responders together for a debriefing. However, some people may be reluctant to sit in a structured setting, but the same principles can be provided, either with one-on-one opportunities or in small groups in a comfortable place of their choosing. People will frequently be very open to discussing the stresses, griefs, pains, and victories while eating a sandwich, drinking coffee, or shifting through the rubble of homes.

D.E. Wolf (1992) notes that disaster and mental health workers seem less threatening when they refer to their services as 'assistance', 'support', or 'talking', rather than announcing themselves as mental health, or even spiritual counselors.

Another technique to help people in a crisis is with spiritual and psychological grounding. It aids in reorienting someone to the "here and now", bringing them back to reality. Grounding skills can help manage overwhelming feelings of intense anxiety. It helps people regain their mental focus from an often intensely emotional state in which they may feel out of control and highly vulnerable. There are two types of awareness and grounding to consider: sensory and cognitive.

Sensory awareness helps survivors by making eye contact. If appropriate, invite them to take your hands. Ask them to place their feet firmly on the ground. Make sure they feel safe and have them look at you in the eyes and slowly breathe in and out with you. Identify non-distressing effects around them that they see, hear, smell, and physically feel. You might find something comforting for them, like holding a pillow, a stuffed animal, something in their hands, or listening to soothing music?

Cognitive awareness is asking questions such as where are you right now? What day of the week is it, what is the year, what is the month, what is the date? What season is it? How old are you? Who is the President of the United States? All these questions are essential to their cognitive health.

A good Scripture to remind them of is *"You can never escape from God's Spirit! You can never get away from His presence!" Psalms 139:7 NLT*

Understand that the Father is with us. We don't know everything, but He does. We must be open to what God wants us to know before every crisis. You can experience stress reactions yourself and they can be physical, emotional, spiritual, cognitive, and interpersonal. As you learn to use these tools in learning to cope with everyday situations you will also have the same tools available to help people understand that although their experience is unique, these are common responses everyone will have in a crisis such as this and just knowing that can significantly reduce anxiety and worry.

Bard & Sangrey (1979) discuss the individual responses to disasters in three stages: the Impact Stage, the Recoil Stage, and Reorganization/Post-Trauma Stage.

In the Impact Stage, the survivor is hit with the reality of what is happening, and the survivor has an automatic stimulus-response that allows him to cope with the catastrophe.

In the Recoil or Withdrawal Stage, there is a temporary suspension of the initial stresses of the disaster. The threat of immediate death is over; the survivors are typically in route to friends, family, or shelter. There is a strong need to seek the companionship of others because sometimes they feel the need to be taken care of.

For example, chaplains might be giving a victim a cup of coffee or a blanket. As the impact begins to hit, survivors may start to express emotions. You will not find that survivors frequently want to share the experience with others, but they'll share more when they begin to attempt to deal emotionally with the victimization of the event.

The Reorganization/Post-Trauma Stage is when you will start to become more fully aware of their losses. Feelings of loss, guilt, and anger may be expressed, and they may ask the "why" question while seeking meaning. Research has shown that people will show resiliency in recovery and bounce back quickly. However, it is also essential to recognize that adverse reactions are common.

The chaplain must first allow a survivor to give voice to their situation and then give confirmation as to what they have said so that they can hear it for themselves. People will speak things that are not true because of perception.

Empathy is the fundamental dimension of helping. It is not apathy or sympathy but really feeling what the other person is feeling. The chaplain must re-create the other person's world by entering their frame of reference and replicating those feelings and thoughts by becoming a rational and emotional mirror. The chaplain cannot truly understand without empathy, which is readily evident to the survivor. When a person listens with empathy, a rapport is built, creating an environment of trust and healing.

A common mistake of chaplains is interrupting survivors too early through their guiding questions. There is a time when this is appropriate during an assessment, but you must be very selective in your interruptions as it can distract people from saying what needs to be said. The chaplain will need to redirect the individual to keep them from falling into a downward emotional spiral. A person's attitude is a statement, both literal and spiritual. It is a process we can witness and decide our position that we will lovingly assume with the people around us. Words are the tools, but there are also power drives from awareness and love.

Here are some crisis counseling mistakes to avoid:

Mistake #1: Trying to advise without listening.
Mistake #2: Condemning instead of understanding.
Mistake #3: Talking too much rather than listening.
Mistake #4: Giving ungodly, unbiblical, worldly advice.
Mistake #5: Not giving the person something to act on.

Spiritual care in crisis is urgent and spontaneous. In most cases, victims have no prior association with the crisis chaplain and have no basis for trust or confidence. Furthermore, the victims rarely have future contact with the crisis chaplains and have difficulty trusting due to the brevity of their relationship.

Crisis Chaplains prioritize stress mitigation through early intervention and releasing ventilation, making the contact without delay, and allowing the victim to "vent". Because they don't provide long-term care Crisis Chaplains are, in effect, "spiritual paramedics."

Spiritual care in the aftermath of critical events and disasters is not necessarily "witnessing," "evangelizing," "preaching," or "proselytizing." During this critical period, spiritual care will be feeding the hungry, clothing the naked, providing water for the thirsty, sheltering the exposed, and caring for the wounded and sick. The practical acts of compassion and caring are the most immediate needs.

Disaster and Crisis Chaplains are highly trained in stress mitigation, trauma response, and victim psychology. Like other chaplain specialties, they are expert listeners and well acquainted with grief therapy and comforting grief. Previous education, training, and experience are the foundations for their ministry in this very specialized setting. However, contemporary global issues and political differences point to the need for supplemental education and training in providing appropriate spiritual care after terrorism, biological warfare, mass casualties, and other horrific disasters.

As a Disaster Chaplain myself, I must take training every year to renew my Foursquare Disaster Relief (FDR) requirements. I use International Critical Incident Stress Foundation, Inc., also known as ICISF for my training. Many agencies like the police and fire departments also use this same training. If you would like to use this resource, their phone number and website for USA training is:

Phone number: (410) 750-9600
Emergency Hotline: (410) 313-2473
Web: ICISF.org

Crisis and Disaster Chaplains are incredibly vulnerable at another level as well. They may feel the added distress of not having answers, not being in charge, and not having the resources to "fix" the vast array of problems they face. They may feel the pressure of having to continue doing the daily and weekly routine tasks of being a local pastor while trying to minister to the needs of victims, relief workers, and relief agencies. They may have difficulty cooperating with leaders of other faith traditions within the community or feel excluded by relief agencies who arrive to help. The media may intrude on their privacy or elevate them to unwelcome celebrity status. Such vulnerability leads to compassion fatigue. Crisis and Disaster Chaplains become emotionally depleted after hearing and experiencing the pain and suffering of victims. They are not tired of being compassionate, but they are tired. They no longer have the emotional energy to be present in people's stories.

Survival skills include basic self-care before, during, and after the event. Setting appropriate boundaries, learning to delegate, and maintaining a personal support system are essential skills for Crisis and Disaster Chaplains. They must be wise enough to excuse themselves from responding to the disaster if need-be.

Perhaps they have recently experienced a death of a loved one or they are recovering from a serious illness or medical treatment. Perhaps they or their immediate family have been victimized. To be effective and helpful during the crisis moment, Chaplains must redefine their ministry expectations to accommodate the circumstances of the disaster and prioritize personal prayer, meditation on the Word, and worship. As the Christian tradition would say, they must remember to abide in the Vine.

"I am the vine, ye are the branches: He that abideth in me, and I in him, the same bringeth forth much fruit: for without Me ye can do nothing." John 15:5

CHAPTER 19
DISASTER CHAPLAINS

According to the United States International Strategy for Disaster Reduction, the frequency of disasters caused by natural hazards has been increasing. On average, 78 disasters per year occurred during the 1970s, and this number grew to 351 per year during the first decade of the new millennium. For example, tragedies such as hurricane Katrina, the BP oil spill in the Gulf of Mexico, the Tsunami in Thailand, the sequenced disasters of nuclear reactors in Northern Japan, and even ongoing warfare and terrorism in Iraq, Syria and our own nation have all happened since the year 2000. We need chaplains to be ready to deploy and serve.

When people experience disappointment or crisis, they often respond with fear, confusion, or anxiety. During these moments of upheaval or distress, people need encouragement. A significant demonstration of healing is giving encouraging well-chosen words and specific ministry action. When all seems hopeless, the chaplain brings the assurance of hope to a despairing soul. People suffering will welcome the chaplain who says, "You're not alone."

I wasn't sure how to handle being a disaster chaplain until my first time out. I knew I would see much devastation and people with much sorrow. I was with Chaplain John Peterson. He was a well-seasoned Disaster Chaplain with Foursquare Disaster Relief.

The first disaster was in Santa Rosa, California. John also had been in Texas during the flooding prior to this fire disaster. I was so glad that Chaplain Shirley Hampton would be with him so I could learn from her as well. I learned I wanted to be a Disaster Chaplain on the very first day.

Some people were so devastated that emotionally they were out of control. After sharing with her what I believed Holy Spirit gave me to share, giving her a shoulder to cry on and mainly listening to her, she was calm in about 30 minutes. Even her husband commented with Chaplain John because he hadn't been able to help her for about a week. I'm not saying she still didn't go through some things, but it was a start.

You see as a chaplain in a disaster you're only there just a few days. It would be best to help them to understand it's not over. Some will be OK, and some will need extra help and counseling. If they belong to a church, they have a Christian family who will also help them through it. It's very lonely if they don't know the Lord because they may not have a family to help them walk through this.

When choosing your words depend on Holy Spirit. It is devastating and unless you've been through things like this, you will never know how they feel losing everything.

Crisis and disaster Chaplains are incredibly vulnerable at another level. They don't have control of everything, and they don't always have the resources to "fix" the vast array of problems. They may feel the pressure of having to continue doing the daily and weekly routine tasks of being a pastor of a church while trying to minister to the needs of victims, relief workers, and relief agencies. They may have difficulty cooperating with leaders of other faith traditions within the community or feel excluded by relief agencies who arrive to help. The media may intrude on their privacy or elevate them to unwelcome celebrity status. Such vulnerability leads to compassion fatigue. Crisis and disaster chaplains can become emotionally depleted. They are not tired of being compassionate, but they are tired. They may find they no longer have the emotional energy to be present in the time of people's needs.

Survival skills for compassion fatigue include basic self-care before, during, and after the event. Setting appropriate boundaries, learning to delegate, and maintaining a personal support system. Disaster chaplains must be wise enough to excuse themselves from responding to every disaster. Perhaps they have recently experienced a death of a loved one or they are recovering from a serious illness or medical treatment. Perhaps they or their immediate family have been victimized. To be effective and helpful during the crisis moment, we must redefine our ministry expectations to accommodate the circumstances of the disaster and prioritize personal prayer, meditation on the Word, and worship. We can't do any of this without abiding in the Vine, Jesus our Lord.

Are you called to be a Disaster Relief Chaplain?

CHAPTER 20
CHAPLAIN SHIRLEY'S STORY

The leader of the group I was with was Chaplain Shirley Hampton, who has an incredible heart for people effected by disasters. If you experience tragedy, I hope you have somebody like Chaplain Shirley to help. God definitely gives her strength for what He's called her to do.

She has given me permission to share with you her story about her road to chaplaincy. God gave her a gift to do this ministry with His heart. You see, not everyone had a perfect life, but God can use us when we surrender what we have to Him.

Chaplain Shirley begins with *2 Corinthians 5:17-18 (NKJV) Therefore, if anyone is in Christ, he is a new creation; old things have passed away; behold, all things have become new. Now all things are of God, who has reconciled us to Himself through Jesus Christ and has given us the ministry of reconciliation.*

Chaplain Shirley continues: God sends people and sometimes even circumstances into our lives that will make us recognize the love He has for us and cause us to desire to be reconciled to Jesus Christ, to live as a new creation.

The blood of the Lamb and the love of my Savior has helped me to overcome the obstacles in my life and has brought me to a relationship with my King; my desire is to take my pain and turn it into His gain. I want to share the word of my testimony with you as I pray – Asking Holy Spirit to use my words.

In 1968 my family attended a Baptist church for just a short time. I remember asking Jesus into my heart, and then my whole family, my mom, my dad, my brother, and I all got baptized at the same time. I remember the feeling of being cleansed, and at seven years old I had a newness in my heart because I had personally asked Jesus into my heart. Unfortunately, after my family and I got saved and baptized, we moved and never attended church as a family again.

I grew up in the suburbs of Sacramento. My dad

continued a truck driving career through the 48 states and was home only a few weeks out of the year. My older brother was my big brother, but when times got tough, he turned to drugs and fighting, and I followed along as the little sister. When I was eleven my parents had another baby, and this new baby boy took all my mom's attention I felt neglected. She had to start working out of the home and would leave my older brother and me to tend to our little brother often.

My heart began to grow cold. I was a lonely child, always missing my dad, feeling like my mom always put all the work of cleaning, cooking, and tending to my younger brother on me, yet at the same time I was trying to be accepted by my older brother. I began experimenting with drugs because I thought the drugs and drinking, would take away the pain, but my heart just got harder and harder, and hate soon dominated my emotions.

At 13 I began "trucking" on the road with my dad. My mom had told me that she loved me as a daughter but hated me as a person. I now know she meant she hated the sinful life I was living but loved me as her daughter, but these words at 13 became my wall. I shut everyone out. I searched for freedom and peace in everything in this world. I thought I had found what I was searching for as I traveled with my dad for the next two years, living on the roads of America through my vulnerable teen years. I now knew the love of my earthly father, but I was his worker, partner, and trucking buddy. I would see the eagle fly far above the earth as we traveled the white line of the roads. I started to feel a spirit, I thought from the eagle. A spirit I did not know but knew there was a spirit with me.

Going to school was the law, and I had to go to high school, but I had experienced so much life out on the road, definitely a different life than high school and I didn't fit in. I had a burning desire to be on the road and soon found that bikers were almost like truckers. I thought I had found freedom being in the wind, but my heart was still lonely and empty, and the drugs, sex, and drinking became my life.

I became involved in the biker lifestyle, partying, living without borders, the club, and the brothers and sisters, we cared for each other. I fit in to this club, known today as gangs, and I belonged. I did things that should have killed me or ruined my soul forever. But each time that I thought I had gone to the pit of hell and was playing in the devil's playground, I would see an eagle flying above me, the eagle I thought had become my spirit. It would bring me hope and a desire to push on and be a different person.

I look back on those days of the past and know it was God, my Father, who protected me and gave me the desire to be better. I even received the nickname "Eagle" because everyone knew I was always under watch and protected.

One night after partying, disgusted with who I had become, feeling so worthless and unloved, running from another violent scene, and myself. I was locked in an outhouse, ready to take my own life. A light came through the crack in the door, but it was in the middle of the night. I peeked out, afraid it might be the law. I saw a church building with a cross on it. I remember crying out to the cross asking, "why don't you love me?"

I became involved with one guy and soon found myself pregnant and forced into marriage by his family. The fairy tale wedding that I had hoped for since a child was broken, I was forced into a marriage that we both were not ready for, but this baby boy was loved. I felt love for the first time. I was able to give love to this baby and through this child God was showing me He loved me!

On my 18th birthday, while in the woods partying with our club, I awoke to a fist hitting my face. My husband had attacked me while I was asleep. My face was severely bruised, my spirit broken, and my self-worth destroyed. I then lived as a whipped puppy, determined to be a submissive wife, doing what my husband asked me to do, indulging in drugs to try and keep the peace. The abuse, both physically and emotionally ruled my life. I had no worth, except for the baby boy who needed me, the love I felt Father God had sent me from heaven to earth.

The 1st time I heard the voice of God was in 1982, at the age of 21. Standing at my kitchen sink, my 2-year-old son came walking into the kitchen with a needle sticking out of his arm saying, "Da Da Daddy," I remember the feeling of something coming over me, and I heard a voice, that said, "*Shirley this is not the life I meant for you to live.*"

Strength grew inside me, and I was determined to make a change. But who was I? I was a 21-year-old girl, 9th-grade dropout, needle tracks on my arms, bruises on my body, a broken spirit, a mother of a 2-year-old son, and branded as a club member? How could I change? How could I get away from this life I had developed?

I knew of the road and of a spirit that gave me strength, the Eagle that flew above. Could this Eagle be a spirit of God calling me to a better life? All I knew was that I heard a voice saying, *"This was not the life that I was meant to live."*

I gathered a plan, slowly hid things of my sons outside, and slipped away in the darkest of the night. I hid my son and myself for over six months, changed my name, and only by the grace of God was I able to get away.

I settled in a little mountain town, no one knowing who I was, or where I came from. I enrolled in college, got my GED, and found myself in an Automotive Technology class, bound and determined to make a good life for my son and me. We rented a home with acreage that my son could run and play on, but we were unable to connect the propane gas line in that old house because over the years the lines had rotted. I was attending college full-time, working two part-time jobs, and restoring a condemned home.

One night in 1984, after living without hot water for more than six months, I was able to re-run all the gas lines and I took a hot shower inside. I was exhausted and fell asleep, my son in his bed, safe in his room. I awoke in the middle of the night to a sound that I thought was a gunshot, but instead, it was the hot water tank about to explode; I threw on my robe and walked out of my bedroom door, and noticed the back of the house was on fire. I ran into my son's room, grabbed my son and ran away from the home that I had built as a safe haven for us.

As I walked further from the house full of smoke, I turned around and saw the explosion that is still fresh in my memory today. What caused the fire? A 1" pipe, that I did not replace, had leaked and the hot water tank blew up. That caused five counties to alarm fire stations, fire trucks, police, and news reporters. I stood outside watching my home blaze, with no shoes on my feet and only a bathrobe around my body.

A firefighter approached me and gave me a Bible I had in the house that my grandmother had given me and a picture of my son, Justin. Something came over me, something powerful, almost like the eagle's wings had surrounded me. I could not comprehend the feeling at the time, but I now know it was the Holy Spirit. The Holy Spirit came upon me, and nothing else mattered. It was all material things. I looked up to the sky and thanked the Lord that this picture of my son was not all I had. I had my son, and he was standing beside me. Safe in the Eagle's wings.

We made the newspaper's front page, and now everyone knew who I was, where I had come from, and what I was doing. But I had determined, I was not going back.

I became more independent that I had ever been, and my heart became even more complex. I finished school as the first lady to ever complete the Automotive Technology program. I was giving my son a good mountain life, keeping a roof over our heads, and raising him the best I could as a single mom. I had built a wall around us that no one could get in. Today I know this was a prison wall that a hard, independent heart and put me in. But that is where I was.

I tried to go to church, but I felt I could never fit in. My guilt and shame of being a single mother, a biker club member, and a drug user kept me isolated. I carried these labels as my heart grew colder and even more challenging.

Again, I thought moving would be the answer to my problems, so I moved to another small mountain town, became an apprentice mechanic, and was determined to make something of myself. My problem was that I was not allowing God to lead me, and I was never going to allow love in my life. I was prideful, independent, and alone.

In 1989 it had been five years since we had lost our home to a fire and another tragedy struck. I had been away for a weekend and as I returned, I drove up to my house that had burned while I was away with yellow tape surrounding it. Detectives were searching for the cause of a fire. My home had burned again, and everything I owned was gone again. I just shook my head and screamed, "no....... not again."

I was then interrogated for hours at these questions about who I was, where I had come from, and who was I associated with. I walked away again with the shirt on my back, my son, and more hatred than I had ever had, more hatred than anyone should ever experience.

I continued at work, living in campsites until I found a new home, but with my hard heart and hatred of life, my son didn't want to be around me anymore. Hatred was growing in his heart as well but directed towards me.

My dad was still driving truck on the open road, and one day he asked me to meet him at a Dairy Queen, which I did. I remember his words so clearly "Shirley, you have never listened to me a day in your life, but you are going to listen to me now. I'm taking you home". He drove that 18-wheeler into the dealership with all those cars around, went up to my boss, and said he was taking my toolbox because he was taking me home. I listened to the only man I had any respect for, and my son and I returned home to live with my mom, Dad, and brother. Back to the same city I had left so long ago and the lifestyle I wanted no part of.

God had spared my life in so many ways at so many different times. I knew of Him now and I had His word that He spoke to me in my heart, and I had personally felt a spiritual experience more than once. I was clean from the drugs and violence, and I started to search for this friend that people had told me about, they called Him Jesus.

I sought after this Jesus and started learning more of His ways, and my heart grew soft for love. I got involved with my family, my mom, my dad, and even my younger brother and I grew fond of my family. I had a good job leading to a solid career, attended a church where I felt accepted and free, had my family, and had freedom from drugs and alcohol. I had become a new person, a new creation in Christ with the hope of life, liberty, and a friendship with Jesus.

I settled into this suburb of the city, the same city in which I had the relationship with the biker's club. But only by the grace and protection of Father God I never have had another encounter with them.

My focus was still on being a single mom. Now, with a teenage boy, I was working in an automotive company as a technical editor, just as my college days had prepared me, and I was succeeding. For the first time in my life, I was appreciated and needed. I had received my strength and spirit back, but this time the heart I knew was not of this eagle that flew above the earth but of Father-God who loved me so much that he sent His Holy Spirit to walk with me.

It had been ten years since I had escaped from my ex-husband and divorced. He went to prison, as I went to college. But one day I opened the door to our home, and there stood my son's father, the man he had never known as a dad. He was clean and was eager to have a life with his son and me and stated that drugs and violence would never happen again. I was tired of being a single mom, always struggling in every area of life. My heart desired to have love, so I let him back into our home and our lives.

My job was doing well, and I was able to put my husband through a career education course so that he could get a job. Soon I became pregnant with our baby girl. One day after the baby was born, he had been out fishing with friends and returned home drunk and he started to threaten my baby girl, who was just crawling. This time, with my spirit back, I stood up to him but was quickly taken down and beaten and broken just as before.

All the softness and love in my heart once again, became bitterness and hatred. The beatings continued, and soon knew no other way to keep the peace in our home but to join him in the drugs and alcohol. I thought my son and daughter needed their dad in their lives, even if we were parents with addictions. I didn't want to raise them alone and I thought I could hide from this burning in my spirit to follow Jesus. I felt this was the only life that I deserved.

In August of 1996, after a day of partying in the hot sun, there were three of us were driving back to the city, but all of us were under the influence. We stopped for a bathroom break, and I wanted to speak up about our condition and stated that we should not be driving. The next thing I knew I was being strangled and someone else was yelling at him, and he stopped and threw me to the ground. I ran and locked myself in a bathroom. As I was lying on the bathroom floor, bleeding, broken, and badly bruised God again spoke to me and said, *"Shirley, this is not the life I intended for you to live."* At that moment, I realized how much God desired to give me a good life. At that moment, I gave my heart to Jesus. I had asked Jesus into my heart 28 years ago, but now, I was ready to surrender and follow Him.

The police came, and as I was getting up from that bathroom floor, I walked out sober, even though I had been drunk. My face had a new countenance. Dino returned to prison that night for attempted murder, and I walked away free. Free from sin, alcohol, drugs, and an abusive husband. This is when I began to follow the instructions from my Savior, My healer, Jesus Christ.

This Jesus, who I now knew, was honest and dependable. He had saved me from a violent attack, he had given me another chance with my life, and He reunited me to my Father-God. So, I wanted to search out His ways and start living by them. I was able to stop the drinking and drugs on the night of my encounter with Jesus because this was an encounter with Love, and I have never returned. For the first time in my life, I was putting Jesus first, I was learning to live life and allow Him to direct my steps. But my heart was still lonely with a desire to be married to a loving man was still apparent.

I had asked the Lord if I could marry a certain man named Duane and God said "no". But I reasoned with Him and said no one could ever love me; I was so broken. Duane was not like any man I had ever known before. He bought me gifts, spoiled my children, and took me places I could never afford. He knew of my past and still loved me. He repeatedly told me that he would never mistreat me. I explained to God how I longed to be a bride and to live right and I reasoned myself right out of God's instruction and into marriage.

Duane gave me the wedding of my dreams, with promises of living in the mountains, away from the city, a life of success. We were married in October however he gave so many excuses of why we couldn't live together yet. Finally, in August of the following year, my 9-year-old daughter and I were allowed to move into his home and that's when life changed.

Drugs and alcohol were hidden around the house, and I found out that he too, was a drug addict. He needed money for home repairs, so he said. So, I took a loan from my 401K. But everyday more was revealed about this man who was now my husband. My heart only knew of real love from my Heavenly Father, yet I had disobeyed Him again, and now I was living a life that was not blessed.

One night in January 2002, Duane was in a rage, throwing things around the house and destroying the walls. He then picked up my daughter's rat cage and threw it, killing the baby rats. At that moment, I knew I had to leave, so my daughter and I got in my car and went to a motel room to hide from the fury.

It wasn't long and I saw the red lights of a police car and I was told that he had accused me of abuse and that I was being arrested for domestic violence. Unbelief clouded my mind, and my heart thought 'this is what I deserve'. My daughter was taken to a safe place, and I was taken to jail. As those cell doors shut with a loud bang, a rushing wind came upon me. It was the baptism with the Holy Spirit, right there in jail. I had peace and joy that the officers could not understand, but I knew God had saved my life again and placed me in a safe place. I surrendered my life again, to God almighty and have never taken it back.

I got out of jail that night and it took almost two years of being stocked and threatened by him, having to have escorts in public places, being in safe houses, losing money and homes to pay for lawyers in order to break free from this man's deception. All charges were finally dismissed on me and placed on him. All glory to God.

God had again shown Himself mighty, even saving me from my disobedience. I was not worthy, but He picked me up, wrapped His arms around me, and gave me His Holy Spirit to guide me. I knew I was protected under His wings. He was that Eagle that flew above me for many years calling me to His kingdom. Jesus pursued me. I was now willing and ready to listen to the only One who truly loved me.

I became involved with a church, serving in children's ministry, and a member of a new gang, a new club called Christians. I attended each time the doors were open, wept at each alter call, and surrendered the life that I had to let God use it as He wills. I wanted to serve Him with everything I had, everything I was and had no clue of where He would take me, but I surrendered to His plan.

A man from the same church tried to court me, but I declined. His name was Stan. I wanted nothing to do with anyone but God. I could not trust, and I thought I could not love. I told Stan my whole story and yet he persisted in being my friend. I soon saw he was a man of God. Stan respected me, but better yet, he respected the Word of God. He loved God more than me, but he also knew God said that I was the girl he would marry. I fought against it but soon realized I was fighting against God's plan for my life again. I explained to God that I had to hear clearly from His throne if I was to marry Stan and God answered and said, "Yes, Stan is the man."

God had made many promises throughout His Word, and as noted in the Old Testament when God asked Abram to "*walk before Me and be blameless*," as indicated in Genesis 17:1, Abram agreed and submitted. So God gave Abram a new name, Abraham. I also was given a new name. I took the name of my God-given husband and was given a new life with again a new beginning. God loved me so much. He knew of my loneliness and my heart's desire to be a bride, not just to have a wedding but to live in holy matrimony. When God changes someone's name, it is either for a character change or a significant call from God. For me it was both.

As the Scriptures say, *"if anyone is in Christ, he is a new creation; old things have passed away; behold, all things have become new."*

I first asked Jesus into my heart at the age of 7, and again 28 years later. I gave Jesus my spirit and six years after, I gave Jesus my life to do with as He pleased.

In 2006, the Lord directed my husband and I to open a small business and He has given us favor and blessing within this community, and even the world, recognizing us as "solid Christian business owners." We work this business knowing it is the Lord's business, and we have succeeded beyond my belief. God has renewed my mind so I can run and operate a profitable business.

In 2009, we became elders at our church. God trusts me and allows me to be a watchman for His servants. A prayer warrior, it's been told that when I pray, the power that God releases through me is like "eagle claws". To God be the Glory.

In 2010, my heart began to cry for the wounded, the lost, and the one's experiencing disaster. God has allowed me to extend His love for those who have just went through a catastrophe. I have been and still am serving as a Disaster Relief Chaplain. I've been deployed to the Oklahoma Tornadoes' and served on almost every one of our California Wildfires. I have walked with people as they return to the devastation that once was their home—cried with loved ones as they said goodbye—encouraged and supported towns as they rebuilt. The love that God has allowed my heart to feel and the ability He has given me to go and serve is beyond my understanding.

I now serve as a Community Chaplain and Red Cross Spiritual Care Worker. God has also asked me to pursue Law Enforcement Chaplaincy, which He is still working out to complete the good work He began.

God has given us all, including you, the ministry of reconciliation. First, we ourselves, are to be reconciled to our Savior Jesus Christ, who came from Heaven to earth, to die on the cross for our sins, as our substitute. Then He has given us new life in His resurrection, a promise fulfilled by the Holy Spirit. He also desires that we become ministers of reconciliation, to tell others what Christ has done for them. God expects us all to live a holy life, just as He is Holy, and I can attest that this can be attained only through daily seeking the Holy Spirit, by surrendering our lives to the perfect plan of our Heavenly Father Who has no harm in store for us and Who will pursue us to the end.

The love of Christ leaves me no choice but to live my life for Him, proclaiming that by faith in Christ, I am a new creation and a servant representing Him.

Chaplain Shirley's story was so compelling that I wanted you to hear it. I hope someday I can be half the chaplain that she is. I have served under Chaplain Shirley three times as of writing this book and it was an honor to work under her and see how God uses her in a mighty way.

CHAPTER 21
MY STORY

Often, in a disaster, people will think they're fine, that they don't need help. Allow me, if you will, to share my crisis story from 1980.

I believed in God, but I wasn't serving Him at this time of my life because I thought God had given up on me because of some stupid things I had done. I didn't understand how great His love for me was, and I certainly didn't understand the blood covenant He made on my behalf.

I had gone to Texas for my grandmother's 90th birthday and my sister went along with me on this road trip so we could drive my new 3-month old motorhome together.

Since I would be in the Dallas area, I decided to make this a business trip as well and pick up a few trailer items we needed for our business in California. While we were in Dallas we stayed with a relative.

My motorhome had a few mechanical problems on the way to Texas and I knew it would not make it back to California. So, I put it in the mechanic's shop. Now the motorhome is with the mechanic for eight days and as close as I am to my relative in Dallas, I didn't say anything about my problems because I was the kind of person that didn't think I needed anyone's help. I wasn't going to lean on anyone or use them as a crutch. I wish I knew then what I know now about needing friends and family. I put my sister on a plane to California because she needed to return to work, and I waited from the motorhome to be repaired.

A few days later, the mechanic called and said the motorhome was fixed so I picked up my beautiful motorhome and headed west out of Dallas. I had traveled only two hours, and was going through Clyde, Texas. I remember that name because that was my husband Willie's real name, although he was known as Willie. The same trouble I had experienced with the motorhome started again. The engine stopped running and so I was preparing to pull over when I looked in the right-hand mirror, and the motorhome was on fire with flames clear to the roof. I'm not in a panic but I know I need to get over and stop. When I did, I didn't exit the driver's door because the fire extinguisher was at the side door of the motorhome, and I needed to grab that to extinguish the fire. (After later sharing the story with my husband, we laughed for years about the fact that I had to put the keys in my pocket as I exited the seat). I grabbed the fire extinguisher and escaped the side door ready to act as a female fire-fighter.

The last thing I remember seeing is the motorhome has gone up in flames, but the driver's door is still intact. Good thing I had the key (chuckle). Several weeks later the insurance adjuster said the fuel line had not been tightened and the motorhome was so saturated with gasoline fuel that no one would have been able to put that fire out with a fire-extinguisher alone.

The police officers showed up on the scene and after the investigation one officer took me to the precinct and called my husband to make sure he understood everything that had happened and to be ready to pick me up at the airport in California. I thought I was remaining calm, but I was not understanding everything, and I thought it was because I was frustrated about the fire and the fact that I had just lost my new motorhome. But now I know it was a bit of PTSD.

The police officer drove me 110 to 120 mph to get me to the small Clyde airport for the last flight back to DFW airport where I could catch a flight home to California. He didn't just drop me off at the airport because he knew something I didn't. He understood I could mentally flip out at any time because of the crisis I had just experienced. So, he made a point of walking to the plane to make sure I got on the plane to DFW. Back in 1980, I'm curious to know how much training people had about PTSD. He wasn't young, probably 40 to 50 years old. But he had an understanding of what could set somebody off that I never understood at that time.

Although I was still frustrated, I remained calm until three days after I had arrived home. I was watching the local news and saw a story of a family, two grandparents and two children, that was driving their motorhome to Magic Mountain in California. The motorhome caught on fire and they were able to get the children out of the motorhome but the grandparents burned to death.

I'm no longer calm; I'm freaking out and I don't know why I'm having such a delayed reaction. My husband Willie understood. He had served in WWII and experienced PTSD when he returned, just like many of our veterans have. So my sweet husband had empathy, he knew how I felt and he knew how to help me calm down.

Willie went on to tell me that diesel doesn't catch fire as quickly as gasoline. In fact, to help me remain calm he went out and purchased a diesel truck for me that I drove for years. I couldn't get in a gas-driven motorhome for years. In fact, I don't think I would ride in one to this day.

As a chaplain, when talking to people in a crisis, don't cause one to be afraid by telling them they could fall apart at any time, but encourage them to talk to their pastor, or neighbors, or a counselor that can help them process what just happened to them.

God had a plan for my life, just as He does for every person. Encourage people to learn from the past but keep moving forward. Most people are happy they are alive when they realize that material things can be replaced.

Even though I lost a motorhome to a fire, I've never lost my home to a fire. So, I don't bring this story up to a person that's just lost their home, I don't know how they feel losing everything. And I trust you'll not use the phrase "I know how you feel". It just doesn't help at the time.

CHAPTER 22
CHAPLAIN KAREN TAVACI'S STORY

Chaplain Karen Tavasci is a Foursquare Disaster Relief Chaplain, Prison and Jail Chaplain, and Red Cross Disaster Spiritual Care Chaplain. This is her story:

During my senior year of high school, we were given an assessment test to help us determine what our career path should be. Because of certain interests in science and compassion levels, I was told I should be a nurse, but not a doctor.

I began nursing school but soon discovered I would make a much better "pink lady" aka: "candy striper", than a nurse. The volunteer that helps at a hospital with simple tasks.

Of course, the assessment test did not have a pastor or chaplain as an option but if it had this is the direction my interests, gifts, and talents would have shown.

Had I known that I would love chaplaincy work before I was married with children, I would have joined the training with Last Days Ministry or Mercy Ships and been doing the work chaplains do all along. Instead, God gave me the privilege of raising my children, teaching, and shepherding them. Then He led me to the Disaster Relief and CISM training through Calvary Chapel and Foursquare Church. It was a great fit with the gifts, talents, and personality that God created me with. It was like I had found my tribe.

Our tribe is like-minded people who are well trained and then deploy to disasters to serve the victims that God so loves. An acquaintance described it as "You are like a dove swooping into places of trauma, bringing healing in your wings"

Because there are lapses of time between disasters, there's some down-time where I'm never sure of what to do with my time. I always feel like I should be doing something. Although I was trained as a Sheriff/Law Enforcement Chaplain, the first door the Lord opened for me was in the local jail. To my surprise, I've been serving in that role ever since.

Chaplains are sometimes called "Urban Missionaries" because they go out into their community serving hospitals, nursing homes, businesses, and more and minister rather than going overseas as in the traditional sense of missionaries. Even pastors cannot cover all the bases in a community but by providing training opportunities to raise up a chaplain force and sending them out anointed and appointed they can bring healing, hope and the presence of Jesus to the hurting because of crisis and disaster.

I make myself available to whatever and wherever the Lord needs me. I'm living in the perfect will of God for me.

When I (Chaplain Patty) met Chaplain Karen, she was an inspiration to me then and is still an inspiration to me today. She's been an encouraging person to all chaplains.

When we arrived in Santa Rosa, California, to help with the fire disaster victims there, we were locked out and told by the Red Cross we could not come in. Please note the Red Cross is not favorable towards Christians or even Christians praying. I don't know how Karen did it, but she opened the door for not only our group to get in and serve, but for the Rapid Response Team with the Billy Graham Association. Karen seems to always have the right demeanor and the right words to say to the right people. We knew every disaster relief team needed access to help and knew God would make a way. Here are some verses to encourage you:

"Be strong and of good courage; fear not, nor be afraid of them: for the Lord, thy God, it is He that goeth with thee; He will not fail thee, nor forsake thee." Deuteronomy 31:6 KJV

"Be strong, courageous, and firm; fear not nor be in terror before them, for it is the Lord your God Who goes with you; He will not fail you or forsake you." Deuteronomy 31:6 AMPC

"Be strong. Take courage. Don't be intimidated. Don't give them a second thought because GOD, your God, is striding ahead of you.

He's right there with you. He won't let you down; he won't leave you."
Deuteronomy 31:6 MSG

I like the words "be strong and courageous". Sometimes when we're in a disaster, and we're not sure of ourselves, or even how to react. But God will not leave us, He'll make a way. This is also how we can encourage people "God will not leave them". You are there for a reason because God put you there. God knows why we're there and how He wants to use us, so trust God during these times.

Our team of chaplains with Foursquare Disaster Relief, provided extra hours of help at the paradise fire in Chico California and FDR has served, and continues to serve in disasters all over the world.

One aspect of FDR that helps so much is we pray together every morning and every evening. Chaplains are only human and the sooner we realize we can't do this without Christ, and without one another, the better we'll be at serving others.

Are you called to be a chaplain?

CONCLUSION

In my research for the writing of this book, I realized how many opportunities there are to serve as a chaplain. In the busy-ness of one's life, not everyone will walk into a church, but the church can walk into their life through the ministry of chaplains.

How many people can we reach with the Good News if we'll just take the time to serve? That's what our Savior did, *"He came not to BE served, but to serve."*

Are you called to be a chaplain? Are you ready?

BIBLIOGRAPHY

Chaplin Karen Tavasci
Chaplain Shirley Hampton
Reverend/Chaplain Marilyn Newberry, D.Th
Chaplin John Peterson

Google
https://www.hcmachaplains.org/what-is-a-chaplain/
https://www.militaryonesource.mil
https://www.thegospelcoalition.org
https://chaplain.org
https://careertrend.com
http://www.icpc4cops.org/chaplaincy-intro/chaplain-qualifications.html
https://prisonchaplaincy.wordpress.com/prison-chaplaincy
https://www.hrrv.org/blog/experiencing-a-hospice-chaplain-visit-part-one/
https://crhcf.org/insights/what-is-a-hospice-chaplain/
http://www.acpe.edu
http://www.icisf.org

Haythorn, Trace Executive Director/CEO ACOR

International Crisis Incident Stress Foundation, Inc.

Paget, Naomi K. & Janet R. McCormack the Work of the Chaplain. Prussia, PA 2006

Pickett, JR., Dr. Earl the Complete Handbook of Christian Chaplain Ministry. Bronx, NY

Ready With a Word, Bible Publishers, 2016

ABOUT THE AUTHOR

Patricia Wileman has been a licensed minister since January 2014. She's a retired business-owner and currently serves as a Convalescent Home Chaplain and a Disaster Relief Chaplain but has a desire to enter the chaplaincy at hospitals. She has one son, one daughter-in-law and one grandson. She lives in the beautiful desert of Mohave County, Arizona.

The only degree she had ever earned was a High School graduation and she always felt she was capable of so much more. So, in her twenties Patty took night courses to be a photographer, worked as a photographer and photofinisher for a time but because she was working so hard to raise her son, as a single mom, she went into construction as a water-tank driver for work sites.

She did remarry, and her husband encouraged her to keep learning as long as she wanted to. So, in her thirties she was certified as a scuba-diver then in her 40's she built her business and was the owner and CEO. In her 50's she earned her instrument rated commercial pilot's license with a seaplane endorsement.

In her 60's she returned to school to receive Christian Education beginning with correspondence college, then her AA, then her BA, and in her 70's she completed her Master of Theology, with an Emphasis in Chaplaincy, through Life Point Christian University in Glendale, AZ.

Although Patty spent her energy as a young person in business and not in the kitchen, today she is baking bread, growing a garden and freeze drying her food to store for her family's future.

Her motto? You have a license to learn.